TALLINN CHRISTMAS TRAVEL GUIDE 2024

ACTIVITIES TO DO AND SAFE ADVENTURES

ANGELA RENNER

Copyright © 2024 Angela Renner

All rights reserved.

No part of this book may be reproduced in any form without written permission from the author, except for brief quotations in a review or scholarly work. This includes electronic, mechanical, photocopying, recording, or any other information retrieval system.

Table of Contents

Introduction.. 3
Chapter One... 7
Arrival in Tallinn... 7
Chapter 2... 16
Tallinn's Christmas Markets....................................... 16
Chapter Three... 29
Exploring Tallinn's Old Town..................................... 29
Chapter Four... 43
The Foodie's Festive Adventure................................ 43
Chapter Five.. 54
Holiday Events and Festivities................................... 54
Chapter Six.. 66
A Family Christmas in Tallinn.................................... 66
Chapter Seven.. 79
Winter Adventures Outside the City.......................... 79
Chapter Eight.. 89
Estonia's Unique Christmas Traditions..................... 89
Chapter Nine... 98
Practical Tips During Christmas in Tallinn................ 98
Chapter Ten.. 125
Where to Stay... 125
Conclusion.. 136

Introduction

Imagine stepping off the plane, feeling the crisp winter air on your face as you enter a city that seems lifted from a snow-dusted fairytale. The cobblestone streets of Tallinn are covered in white, and as you begin to wander. The soft glow of Christmas lights spills from the windows of medieval buildings. This is Tallinn during the holidays—where history and winter weave together in a way that few places in the world can match. But don't just take it from me; this guide will be your personal compass through Tallinn's unique holiday season. It is to make sure you experience it in a way that feels both immersive and deeply personal.

First things first, let's talk about arrival. It's easy to find your way to the heart of the city from Tallinn Airport. Whether you opt for the efficient public tram, a quick taxi ride, or something more adventurous like renting a car, getting to the city center is straightforward. But once you get there, Tallinn begins to unfold—one snow-capped corner at a time.

You'll likely start in Tallinn's Old Town, a UNESCO World Heritage site that holds the key to the city's medieval past. During the

Christmas season, this part of the city transforms into something beyond its usual historical allure. You'll be greeted by the towering Christmas tree at Town Hall Square, surrounded by one of Europe's most famous Christmas markets. Stalls selling handmade wool sweaters, intricately crafted ornaments, and steaming cups of mulled wine will call to you from every direction. But there's more to this market than just souvenirs—each vendor has a story, rooted in local tradition, adding layers of meaning to what you bring home.

As you walk through the market, follow the smell of gingerbread and spices. Tallinn's holiday treats are a chapter all their own. Whether you're nibbling on fresh pastries from one of the market stalls or sitting down in a cozy café with a slice of kringel (a local spiced bread), food will be a central part of your Christmas adventure. But it's not just about the food—every bite tells a deeper story of Estonian holiday customs that have been passed down through generations.

And then there's the atmosphere. There you'll walk through narrow lanes where every building seems like it has a secret history, each one now illuminated with holiday lights.

Church bells echo faintly through the crisp air, and on certain evenings, you'll stumble upon carolers singing traditional songs in Estonian. It's easy to lose track of time here—one moment you're exploring alleyways lined with hidden shops, the next you're standing before one of Tallinn's grand cathedrals, its towering spires cutting through the winter sky. But this isn't a journey to rush through; it's one to savor, step by step.

For the adventurers among you, Tallinn offers more than just a pretty backdrop. Step outside the city, and you'll find sprawling snow-covered landscapes, perfect for day trips into nature. From husky sledding to snowshoeing in Estonia's national parks, Tallinn is the gateway to a winter experience that's as diverse as it is unforgettable.

This guide isn't just about ticking off boxes or checking landmarks from a list. It's about letting you in on the little-known secrets and local traditions that make Tallinn's Christmas season unique. By the end of your journey, Tallinn will feel like more than just a destination—it will feel like a place that you've truly come to understand. So, get ready to uncover a different side of Christmas, one that's both rooted in history and filled with the cozy spirit of winter. Welcome to Tallinn, and welcome to your next holiday adventure.

Chapter One

Arrival in Tallinn

Navigating the Airport and Transportation Options

Once you've picked up your bags, there are several convenient transportation options waiting to take you to the parts of Tallinn. Whether you prefer something quick or more budget-friendly, Tallinn's well-organized system has you covered.

The tram is a fantastic option for those who want a seamless connection to the city center. The airport is directly linked to the tramline via the Line 4 route, which takes you to Viru Keskus, the main hub in the city, in just under 15 minutes. The tram stop is located just outside the airport terminal — an easy find once you're through the sliding glass doors. Tickets can be bought from machines at the stop or through an app, making it convenient even for travelers without any local currency yet.

If you're carrying heavy luggage or just want something faster, taxis are available right outside the arrivals hall. Tallinn taxis are affordable compared to other European capitals, and the journey to the center takes only about 10 minutes depending on traffic. Be sure to use a licensed taxi service to avoid any potential price issues — most official taxis have visible pricing meters and the drivers are generally friendly and knowledgeable. If you'd rather use a rideshare service, Bolt, which originated in Estonia, is a popular and reliable option for locals and visitors alike. With just a few taps on your phone, you'll be picked up and on your way in no time.

For those who prefer to drive themselves, the car rental desks at the airport offer a variety of vehicles to suit different needs. Renting a car gives you the freedom to explore not just Tallinn but the surrounding countryside and even nearby cities like Tartu or Pärnu. Winter roads in Estonia are well-maintained, though it's important to note that icy conditions can make driving tricky if you're not used to it. Be sure to request a vehicle with winter tires and consider renting a GPS system for easy navigation.

First Impressions

The medieval architecture, dusted with snow, feels like something out of time. It's as if the city is wrapped in winter's quiet beauty, ready to reveal its hidden corners to those willing to explore.

The first thing you might notice is the Old Town's spires peeking above the skyline, pointing towards a sky that's often overcast but occasionally reveals streaks of pale winter sunlight. Tallinn's Old Town is not only a UNESCO World Heritage Site, but it also feels especially fitting for the festive season. Its cobbled streets, narrow alleyways, and high stone walls look even more inviting when they're covered in fresh snow. As you drive or tram your way closer, the festive lights become more noticeable, glowing softly along streets and around windows, hinting at the celebrations ahead.

On your way to the city center, take a moment to observe Tallinn's mix of medieval and modern. To one side, you'll see towering glass office buildings and sleek shopping centers, a nod to the city's growing reputation as a tech hub. On the other side, the ancient stone walls and towers of Toompea Hill remind you that this city has stood for centuries, braving winters and wars, and yet remains beautifully intact.

Checking into Cozy Christmas-Themed Hotels

After navigating your way into the city and soaking in the first sights of Tallinn, it's time to settle into your accommodations. Luckily, Tallinn has a fantastic selection of hotels that embrace the Christmas spirit, offering warmth and comfort after a long day of exploring.

If you're staying within the Old Town, you'll find plenty of cozy, Christmas-themed boutique hotels nestled among the historic buildings. Places like the Schlössle Hotel and The Three Sisters offer not only luxurious rooms but also a chance to feel immersed in the holiday atmosphere from the moment you step through their doors. These hotels are often housed in centuries-old buildings, so you get a blend of historical charm with modern comfort. Picture sitting by a crackling fire in a cozy lounge, sipping on hot mulled wine as you watch the snow gently fall outside — it's the perfect way to unwind.

For travelers looking for something more budget-friendly without sacrificing the festive atmosphere, there are plenty of options like the Hotel St. Barbara or the Hestia Hotel Barons Old Town. These hotelscombined affordability with comfort, offering rooms decorated with warm colors, soft bedding, and Christmas lights to get you into the festive mood. And because they're located so centrally, you'll always be just a short walk away from the main attractions, like the famous Town Hall Square Christmas Market.

Many of these hotels also go above and beyond with their holiday decorations. You'll often find Christmas trees in the lobby, and some places even offer special holiday packages that include seasonal meals, festive drinks, and tickets to local Christmas events. Whether you're staying in a five-star boutique or a budget-friendly inn, the feeling of being welcomed into a warm, inviting space after a cold day of exploring the city is something Tallinn's hotels do exceptionally well.

From the airport to the first few hours in the city, Tallinn sets the stage for a memorable holiday trip. The ease of transportation, the striking winter scenery, and the cozy hotels all combine to create a welcoming atmosphere for any traveler, whether you're visiting for the first time or returning to experience the magic of Christmas all over again.

A Stroll Through the Illuminated Old Town

Picture this: cobblestone streets covered in a fresh layer of snow, towering medieval buildings draped with twinkling lights, and the soft hum of holiday carols in the air. This isn't just any part of Tallinn—it's the heart of the city, a UNESCO World Heritage site that stands as one of Europe's best-preserved medieval towns. And during Christmas, it feels like a living, breathing postcard from centuries past.

Walking through Old Town is like reading a book where history leaps off the pages. Start at the Town Hall Square, the epicenter of Christmas festivities. This is where the famous Tallinn Christmas Market is held each year, and even though it's bustling with stalls selling traditional goods and festive treats, the history surrounding you is impossible to miss. The Town Hall, a Gothic masterpiece from the 13th century, looms large, with its spire reaching into the sky. During the holiday season, this square is home to Estonia's grandest Christmas tree—a tradition that dates back to 1441, making it one of the earliest documented Christmas tree displays in the world.

When passing through the narrow alleyways, you'll come across medieval merchant houses, churches like St. Olaf's, and fortifications that tell stories of Tallinn's strategic importance throughout history. The lights that adorn the town during Christmas might make it feel festive, but there's something about the age-old stone buildings that remind you of the generations of people who have walked these same streets, perhaps experiencing the same sense of wonder. And in the stillness of the night, when the crowds thin out and the streets become quieter, you can almost hear whispers of the past carried on the cold winter wind.

Local Greetings and Etiquette

Tallinn may have embraced modern tourism, but when it comes to local customs, traditions still play a significant role. Estonians are known for being reserved but warm once they get to know you, so making a good first impression can set the tone for your interactions throughout your stay. As you navigate the holiday festivities, keeping a few local etiquette tips in mind will help you blend in and show respect for local culture.

First and foremost, when greeting someone in Estonia, don't be surprised if the interaction is short and to the point. A simple "Tere!" (hello) will suffice, and when meeting someone new, a firm handshake with eye contact is the preferred method of introduction. Hugging and overly enthusiastic greetings are not typical unless you've developed a close relationship with the person. Even during the festive season, Estonians tend to avoid exaggerated displays of affection or emotion in public.

Once you've made your introduction, don't rush to ask personal questions. Estonians value their privacy, so it's best to steer conversations toward neutral topics like the weather, holiday traditions, or the city's history before delving into anything more personal. One way to leave a positive impression is to show genuine interest in their customs, especially during Christmas. Asking about local traditions, like the holiday meal of verivorst (blood sausage) or the tradition of visiting a sauna on Christmas

Eve, can lead to rich conversations and a deeper connection with the people you meet.

When shopping at the Christmas Market or dining in a restaurant, be sure to remain polite but not overly chatty. Estonians appreciate efficiency, so whether you're ordering food, buying souvenirs, or asking for directions, keep it concise and respectful. A warm thank you—"Aitäh!"—is always appreciated, and leaving a small tip (around 5-10%) in restaurants is considered polite but not mandatory.

Be mindful of personal space, particularly in crowded holiday areas. Estonians value their physical space, so maintaining a comfortable distance is important. Whether you're in line for mulled wine or navigating the streets, being aware of this subtle cultural difference can help you avoid any unintentional awkwardness.

Chapter Two

Tallinn's Christmas Markets

Town Hall Square

Imagine stepping into a scene straight out of a snow-dusted postcard. That's the feeling you get when you wander into Tallinn's Town Hall Square during the Christmas season. Nestled in the heart of the city's Old Town, this historic square transforms into a festive wonderland, where the traditions of the past blend seamlessly with the holiday spirit of the present. The square itself, with its cobbled stones and medieval backdrop, gives you a sense of stepping back in time.

At the center of this bustling square is the towering Christmas tree—said to be one of the oldest public Christmas tree displays in Europe. It's a towering symbol of the holiday, beautifully decorated with lights and ornaments that give a cozy glow in the early evening twilight. Around the tree, wooden stalls are set up in neat rows, each one offering something special for the curious traveler. The stalls range from food vendors serving piping hot mulled wine and warm gingerbread cookies to artisans selling handcrafted goods, every detail capturing the spirit of an Estonian Christmas.

But it's more than just a market—it's a gathering place. Locals and visitors alike gather here to chat, shop, and enjoy performances by choirs singing traditional carols. There's a warmth in the air, not just from the glowing lights or the mulled wine, but from the sense of community that fills the square. The cold air seems to vanish as you take in the sights, sounds, and smells around you.

For history buffs, it's fascinating to know that this square has been the centerpiece of Tallinn's public life for centuries. The medieval Town Hall, which still stands proud, is one of the oldest in Northern Europe. If you're lucky, you might even catch a glimpse of the old Town Hall's dragon-shaped weathervane or step inside for a quick peek at its Gothic interiors. The Town Hall Square becomes more than just a place to shop—it's a living monument that adds depth to your holiday experience.

Handicrafts: Best Local Gifts

One of the great joys of visiting Tallinn's Christmas Market is the chance to bring home something truly unique. The city's local artisans put great care and craftsmanship into their creations, and it shows in every piece you'll find here. Whether you're looking for a keepsake for yourself or the perfect gift for a loved one, Tallinn's market offers treasures that go beyond the ordinary.

Handicrafts and Ornaments

Start with the intricate handicrafts and ornaments that capture the essence of an Estonian Christmas. Local craftsmen carve wooden ornaments in traditional designs, often depicting rural life or mythical creatures from Estonia's folklore. These aren't your mass-produced, run-of-the-mill decorations—they're carefully made with the hands and hearts of the artisans, giving each piece a story of its own. You'll also find glass-blown ornaments, where delicate patterns are etched into fragile bulbs, creating something personal and timeless for your Christmas tree back home.

What makes these ornaments special is not just their beauty, but the craftsmanship behind them. Estonia has a long tradition of woodworking, and each piece reflects that heritage. It's not hard to imagine the workshops where these ornaments are made, often in small family-run businesses that have passed down techniques for generations.

Estonian Wool Products
Next on your list of must-have gifts should be Estonian wool products, which are as practical as they are beautiful. Estonia is known for its high-quality wool, and the market is filled with knitted goods that will keep you warm during the coldest winter nights. The knitwear here is a testament to Estonia's long tradition of wool craftsmanship, and you'll find a variety of items, from thick, cozy sweaters to soft scarves and mittens.

Many of the patterns you'll come across in these woolen goods have deep roots in Estonia's cultural history. Geometric shapes, snowflakes, and traditional motifs woven into the fabric reflect the region's folklore and heritage. The colors range from muted earth tones to bright reds and blues, making each item unique. Some of the most popular items include thick wool socks—perfect for winter evenings—or beautifully patterned mittens, often knit using ancient techniques. Each piece is a reflection of the surrounding landscapes and the harsh winters that shaped the culture here.

As you browse, you'll notice that the wool used in these garments comes from local sheep, and that eco-friendly practices are often a priority for the artisans. Not only are you taking home a piece of Tallinn's Christmas spirit, but you're also supporting sustainable craftsmanship.

Where to Find Them
While you'll find wool products and handicrafts throughout the market, some of the best stalls are run by artisans who specialize in these traditional crafts. Take your time to explore the smaller, tucked-away booths where you can chat with the makers themselves. Many of them are happy to share the stories behind their creations, giving you an even deeper connection to the items you choose to buy.

Holiday Treats

Stepping into Tallinn during the Christmas season feels like entering a world where festive flavors take center stage. It's the tantalizing aromas of mulled wine and freshly baked gingerbread that will truly welcome you. If you're the type of traveler who loves to indulge in local delicacies, Tallinn's Christmas markets are a culinary wonderland.

Let's start with mulled wine, a holiday staple in Estonia, known locally as glögi. As soon as you take your first sip, you'll realize why it's such a beloved winter drink. Served warm and fragrant with spices like cinnamon, cloves, and cardamom, mulled wine is the perfect antidote to the chilly Baltic air. What's more, you can find variations of glögi that include rum or even a splash of local berry liqueur, adding a bold kick. Wander through the Old Town market, cup in hand,

and stop at different stalls to taste each vendor's version—no two are exactly the same.

Let's not forget gingerbread, or piparkoogid, as the Estonians call it. These intricately shaped and beautifully decorated cookies are found at almost every market stall. In fact, gingerbread baking is an art form in Estonia. You'll find everything from simple star-shaped cookies to elaborate, hand-painted masterpieces. Take a moment to watch local bakers at work—it's fascinating to see the precision and creativity they put into each cookie. If you're feeling adventurous, many stalls offer DIY gingerbread kits, allowing you to try your hand at decorating your own.

Aside from the iconic mulled wine and gingerbread, Estonia's Christmas food culture extends far beyond the basics. Look for verivorst, a traditional Estonian blood sausage that's typically served with sauerkraut and lingonberry sauce. While it might not be everyone's go-to holiday dish, it's a must-try for those seeking an authentic Estonian experience. You'll also encounter hot pastries filled with savory meats or cheese, perfect for snacking while exploring the market.

Then there's the sweet indulgence of Vana Tallinn, a locally crafted liqueur that tastes like Christmas in a bottle. With hints of vanilla, citrus, and spices, this drink is often sipped after a hearty meal or mixed into coffee for an extra winter treat. Make sure to buy a bottle to take home—it's one of the best ways to relieve the taste of Tallinn's festive season long after your trip has ended.

Hidden Gems in the Markets

While Tallinn's Town Hall Square is the best of the Christmas markets, the real treasures are often found in the smaller, less obvious corners. Strolling through the bustling market, you'll notice that some stalls pull larger crowds, but it's the quieter ones that hold the most unique finds.

One such gem is a small stall tucked away on the side streets, offering handmade Estonian wool goods. Not your average winter accessories, these items are crafted with traditional techniques passed down through generations. From thick woolen mittens adorned with intricate patterns to scarves made from the softest local wool, these stalls showcase the best of Estonia's textile traditions. And the best part? The vendors are often the artisans themselves, happy to chat about their work and offer insights into the craft. It's worth noting that these wool products aren't just practical—they make for thoughtful and high-quality souvenirs.

Another under-the-radar vendor to seek out is a family-run stall that specializes in hand-carved wooden ornaments. Unlike the mass-produced items you might find in larger stores, these wooden pieces are truly one-of-a-kind. Crafted from local wood, each ornament is meticulously carved to depict Estonian folklore, local wildlife, or scenes from Tallinn's medieval past. The care that goes into these creations is evident in every detail. Whether you're looking for a tree ornament or a small figurine, these handcrafted items carry a bit of Estonia's heritage in them.

If you're a fan of local art, make sure to visit stalls that showcase ceramics and pottery. Estonian artisans are known for their simple yet elegant designs, often inspired by nature. You'll find everything from handmade mugs perfect for your morning coffee to ceramic bowls that make excellent gifts. Some vendors even offer personalized pieces, which add a special touch to your purchase.

Lastly, keep an eye out for the beekeepers selling their honey-based products. Estonia has a strong beekeeping tradition, and the Christmas market is the perfect place to discover the different flavors of local honey.

Some stalls offer honey infused with herbs or spices, while others sell beeswax candles or honey-based skincare products. These stalls are often overlooked, but the quality of their products is exceptional. If you're lucky, the vendor might even give you a taste of fresh honey straight from the comb.

Christmas Souvenirs: What to Buy and Where to Find Them

Shopping for souvenirs in Tallinn during Christmas isn't just about picking up a trinket—it's about taking home a piece of Estonian culture. The markets are brimming with unique, locally made items that make for thoughtful gifts and personal keepsakes.

One of the top items you'll want to bring home is Estonian wool. As mentioned earlier, the country is known for its high-quality woolen goods. Mittens, hats, and scarves featuring traditional patterns are both functional and beautiful. You can find these in abundance at the main Christmas market, but for something truly special, head to smaller craft shops or artisan stalls. These pieces not only keep you warm but also tell the story of Estonia's rich textile history.

For those who appreciate handcrafted jewelry, Tallinn's Christmas market is a haven for finding pieces made from Baltic amber. This ancient fossilized tree resin is found along the Baltic coast, and it's been used in jewelry for centuries. You'll find everything from simple pendants to elaborate earrings, each with its own distinctive amber hue. Whether you're buying it as a gift or for yourself, Baltic amber jewelry makes for a unique and meaningful souvenir.

Hand-carved wooden items are another great find. Whether you're interested in kitchen utensils, ornaments, or decorative pieces, the craftsmanship is impeccable. Look for vendors selling traditional Estonian wooden spoons, cutting boards, or intricately carved boxes. These items are not only functional but also carry a timeless quality, making them perfect gifts for friends and family.

If you're looking to bring home a taste of Estonia, consider buying a bottle of Vana Tallinn liqueur. This sweet, spiced liqueur is a local favorite, and it's perfect for sipping on a cold winter's night. Most market stalls offer beautifully packaged bottles, making them an ideal gift for anyone who enjoys fine spirits.

Pick up a few Christmas ornaments. From delicate glass baubles to hand-painted wooden decorations, the markets are filled with ornaments that will remind you of your time in this festive city. Many stalls offer personalized options, where artisans will write your name or a special message on the ornament, creating a truly one-of-a-kind keepsake.

Chapter Three

Exploring Tallinn's Old Town

UNESCO's Heritage Site

Tallinn's Old Town, a UNESCO World Heritage Site, is one of the best-preserved medieval cities in Europe, and it invites you to explore it at your own pace.

Start at Town Hall Square, where the Town Hall stands as a proud symbol of Tallinn's medieval past. Built in the 1400s, it's the only remaining Gothic-style town hall in Northern Europe. During the Christmas season, this square transforms into a bustling hub filled with seasonal stalls, but even without the markets, it's a sight to behold. Take a moment to admire the spire that reaches toward the sky, topped with the weather vane known as "Old Thomas," Tallinn's guardian since the Middle Ages.

Walking up the winding streets, you'll come across the Alexander Nevsky Cathedral, an iconic Orthodox church with its striking domes.

This building isn't just about its imposing exterior. Step inside to experience the serene atmosphere, where candles flicker and silence offers a brief retreat from the busyness outside.

Don't miss St. Catherine's Passage, a narrow alley that feels like you've stumbled into another time. Along the passage, you'll find artisans working on ceramics, glass, and other crafts, keeping alive traditions that have been passed down through generations.

As you climb Toompea Hill, take a moment to pause and look back at the sweeping view of the Old Town's rooftops. At the top, Toompea Castle stands as a fortress that has witnessed centuries of political changes. Now, it houses Estonia's Parliament, blending its historic roots with the country's modern identity.

Tallinn's Famous Landmarks

Tallinn's Old Town during the holiday season has three landmarks that stand out in the crisp winter air: Alexander Nevsky Cathedral, St. Olaf's Church, and Toompea Castle. These places are more than just architectural marvels; they each hold stories that span centuries, deeply intertwined with the history and culture of this medieval city. In this guide, I'll walk you through their historical significance and what makes them so integral to your Tallinn Christmas journey.

Alexander Nevsky Cathedral

Perched atop Toompea Hill, Alexander Nevsky Cathedral is hard to miss. Its onion domes, rising like sentinels above the Old Town, offer a striking silhouette against the snow-covered skyline. Built during the Russian Empire's rule over Estonia, the cathedral was completed in 1900 and named after a revered Russian military leader and saint, Alexander Nevsky. Its origins are as political as they are spiritual, marking the influence of Russian Orthodoxy on Estonia.

Entering the cathedral feels like stepping back in time. The interior is adorned with intricate mosaics and icons, golden altars, and rich murals that depict various scenes from Orthodox Christian traditions. The air is filled with the scent of incense, and during the Christmas season, the cathedral becomes even more lively with services that draw the local Orthodox community. It's a place where you can truly appreciate the role religion has played in shaping Tallinn's history and culture. If you happen to visit during one of the services, the sound of the choir's chanting is an experience that lingers with you long after you leave.

St. Olaf's Church

From Alexander Nevsky, make your way down the hill toward St. Olaf's Church, one of Tallinn's most iconic structures. Once the tallest building in the world during the Middle Ages, its steeple reaches a dizzying height of over 120 meters. There's a legend that says the church was built in honor of King Olaf II of Norway, but the real allure lies in its evolving role over centuries.

Originally constructed in the 12th century, St. Olaf's has survived fires, lightning strikes, and the test of time. Its Gothic architecture stands as a reminder of Tallinn's medieval past, and during Christmas, the church is a beacon of light amidst the dark, cold days of winter. Climbing to the top of the tower is not for the faint-hearted, but the reward is spectacular—panoramic views of the city's rooftops dusted with snow and the Baltic Sea shimmering in the distance. Inside, the church maintains a simpler, more austere beauty compared to the lavish Alexander Nevsky Cathedral, but its soaring ceilings and massive stone walls evoke a sense of peace and reflection.

Toompea Castle

Just a short walk from St. Olaf's Church, you'll find Toompea Castle, a fortress that has stood guard over Tallinn since the 9th century. Today, it houses the Estonian Parliament, but its layered history stretches back to ancient Estonia, when it was first built as a wooden stronghold by local tribes.

Toompea Castle has been witness to many of Estonia's historical turning points—from the medieval rulers of the Danish and German orders to the rise and fall of the Soviet Union. The pink Baroque facade you see today is a relatively recent addition from the 18th century, but parts of the older medieval structure remain visible. Walking around the grounds, you can imagine the knights and rulers who once called this fortress home. During the Christmas season, the square in front of the castle is often quieter, a contrast to the bustling markets below in the Old Town. It's a place to pause, take in the layers of history around you, and appreciate how these structures have not only survived but evolved with the times.

The Best Photo Spots

If you're wondering where to capture the best moments for your memories or social media, I've got you covered with some must-visit spots that encapsulate the essence of Christmas in Tallinn.

Town Hall Square
Let's start with the heart of it all—Town Hall Square, the pulsating hub of Christmas in Tallinn. The medieval backdrop of the Town Hall, standing proud in the center of the square, instantly makes for an impressive photo. But it's not just the architecture; the Christmas market that springs to life here, with its wooden stalls, glimmering lights, and towering Christmas tree, makes this spot particularly magical during the holidays. Head here during the golden hour, when the daylight begins to fade, and the soft glow of the lights adds a cozy touch to your photos.

St. Olaf's Church Viewpoint
If you're after a bird's-eye view of Tallinn's Old Town in its full festive glory, make your way to St. Olaf's Church. The climb to the top might be a bit challenging, but the view is absolutely worth it. From up here, you can capture the sprawling rooftops of the medieval city dusted with snow, illuminated by the soft winter light. If you go at the right time, you'll catch the Christmas markets buzzing below, surrounded by the ancient architecture that makes this city so unique.

Viru Gate
If you love a mix of historical significance and seasonal decoration, Viru Gate is your go-to. Standing at the entrance of the Old Town, the gate's two towers create a dramatic entry point to the medieval streets within. During the Christmas season, the towers are often adorned with festive decorations, making this an ideal shot to capture the contrast between Tallinn's rich history and the vibrancy of the Christmas season.

Patkuli Viewing Platform
This one's a favorite among locals and visitors alike. The Patkuli Viewing Platform offers a panoramic view of Tallinn's Old Town that

feels almost surreal, especially when the city is blanketed in snow. In the foreground, you'll see the medieval walls and towers, and further out, the modern city peeks through, blending old and new. The soft light of winter mornings or late afternoons turns this into a dreamy spot for photos, and if you're lucky, you might catch a light snowfall adding extra depth to your shots.

The Stories Behind Tallinn's Architecture

Tallinn's medieval architecture isn't just aesthetically pleasing—it holds centuries of stories, legends, and secrets waiting to be uncovered. As you wander through the cobbled streets, you'll begin to notice that every building, tower, and alleyway seems to carry a story of its own. Let me walk you through a few of the most intriguing ones.

The Town Hall Tower
The Tallinn Town Hall, with its tall spire, isn't just an architectural marvel; it's a beacon of the city's past. Legend has it that the dragon figure atop the spire, known as "Old Thomas," has protected the city for centuries. Old Thomas is said to represent the spirit of a brave young

soldier who defended Tallinn in its early days. Today, the figure watches over the town, especially during the festive season, when the square below is bustling with life.

St. Catherine's Passage

There's something mysterious about St. Catherine's Passage. This narrow, cobbled alleyway is lined with the remains of old tombstones and ancient stone walls, remnants of the

13th-century Dominican Monastery. The passage feels like stepping back in time, and according to local legend, it's said to be haunted by the monks who once lived there. While you're here, stop to admire the medieval craftsmanship of the stonework and imagine the quiet life of the monks who once roamed these very streets.

Toompea Castle
Perched on the highest point of Tallinn, Toompea Castle is more than just a fortress—it's the center of political power in Estonia, housing the Estonian Parliament today. But centuries ago, it was the setting for some fascinating tales. One of the most famous legends associated with Toompea is the story of Linda, the mythical wife of Kalev, a giant from Estonian folklore. It's said that she built the mound where the castle stands today, stone by stone, after her husband's death. The mound, named after her, forms part of Tallinn's skyline, and her statue can be found nearby.

Alexander Nevsky Cathedral
Built in the 19th century, this grand Orthodox cathedral sits atop Toompea Hill, dominating the landscape with its impressive onion domes. While it stands as a symbol of Russian

influence over Estonia, the cathedral has a deeper meaning. Some locals used to believe that the cathedral was built deliberately to overshadow the nearby Toompea Castle, a reminder of the country's complex history under different rulers. Today, the cathedral is one of the most photographed sites in Tallinn, especially during the winter season, when its domes glisten under a blanket of snow.

Seasonal Events in Old Town

If there's one thing you don't want to miss during your Christmas trip to Tallinn, it's the array of seasonal events that bring the Old Town to life. From traditional concerts in historic churches to medieval-style performances in open squares, Tallinn knows how to celebrate Christmas with a mix of heritage and entertainment.

Christmas Concerts in St. Nicholas' Church
St. Nicholas' Church (Niguliste), with its Gothic architecture, offers a perfect setting for Christmas concerts. During the holiday season, the church hosts a series of classical music performances that transport you back in time. The acoustics in the church are phenomenal, and the soft glow of candlelight adds to the

atmosphere. Whether it's a local choir singing traditional Christmas carols or a symphony orchestra performing classical works, attending a concert here is a deeply moving experience.

Medieval Plays and Reenactments
Tallinn's medieval heritage isn't just preserved in its architecture—it's brought to life through seasonal performances. One of the most popular events in the Old Town during Christmas is the reenactment of historical tales and legends by performers dressed in medieval attire. You might come across a reenactment of ancient market scenes or short plays performed in the streets, giving you a glimpse of what life

in Tallinn might have been like centuries ago. These performances are often spontaneous, adding an element of surprise to your stroll through the city.

Christmas Markets: Live Music and Folk Dances

At the Christmas markets, particularly in Town Hall Square, the air is filled with festive music. Traditional Estonian folk dances are often performed around the central Christmas tree, accompanied by live bands playing local music. These performances are a wonderful way to experience Estonia's cultural traditions firsthand. If you're feeling brave, you might even join in one of the traditional circle dances, learning the steps from the locals.

Chapter Four

The Foodie's Festive Adventure

Traditional Estonian Christmas Dishes

Tallinn is a city that wears its history and traditions proudly, and nowhere is this more apparent than in its food. Estonian Christmas cuisine, deeply rooted in centuries-old customs, offers a hearty, flavorful experience that feels like a warm hug during the cold winter months. When you arrive in Tallinn, you're greeted not only by the festive lights and markets but also by the unmistakable aroma of traditional holiday dishes that seem to call out from every kitchen and street corner. Let's take a closer look at what makes Estonian Christmas food unique and where you can indulge in these winter feasts around the city.

Sauerkraut and Blood Sausage

If there's one dish that defines the Estonian Christmas table, it's sauerkraut. But this isn't your typical sauerkraut. Estonian sauerkraut is slow-cooked to perfection, often with chunks of pork or ham for added flavor. The result is a deeply savory dish, tangy yet rich with a subtle sweetness that makes it perfect alongside heavier meats. It's a staple, often piled high on plates at Christmas dinners and holiday gatherings.

And then there's blood sausage—verivorst—which may sound intimidating to some, but for Estonians, it's a beloved holiday tradition. Made with barley, blood, and spices, these sausages are typically pan-fried until crisp on the outside, revealing a soft, flavorful interior. Blood sausage is often served with lingonberry jam, the tartness of the berries providing a delightful contrast to the richness of the sausage. It's a dish that speaks to the country's farming roots, using every part of the animal in a way that respects tradition and sustainability.

But don't let the simplicity fool you—these dishes are packed with flavors that warm both body and soul, and they're an essential part of any Estonian Christmas feast.

Other Must-Try Christmas Dishes

One popular item is sealiha, a roast pork dish often served with potatoes and gravy. The pork is typically slow-cooked until it's tender enough to fall apart, making it the perfect accompaniment to the tangy sauerkraut and crispy blood sausage.

Potatoes in various forms are a constant presence, with roasted, mashed, or even fried versions appearing in abundance. And while Estonians love their meats, they don't forget about fish. Sült, a cold meat jelly typically made with pork or beef, is a dish many locals grew up eating at Christmas. Its gelatinous texture may be an acquired taste for some, but it's a festive tradition that goes back generations.

For something on the sweeter side, Estonian Christmas bread—piparkoogid—is a spiced gingerbread that fills homes with the scents of cinnamon, cloves, and cardamom. These cookies are often shaped into stars, snowflakes, and other festive designs, perfect for nibbling with a cup of mulled wine, or glögi.

Tallinn's Top Restaurants for Christmas Feasts

When visiting Tallinn during the Christmas season, you'll find no shortage of places to sample these traditional dishes. Many of the city's restaurants embrace the holiday spirit with special Christmas menus that highlight local ingredients and time-honored recipes.

1. Olde Hansa

If you want to immerse yourself in Tallinn's medieval atmosphere, head to Olde Hansa. This restaurant got your back, serving up a medieval-inspired feast in a candlelit setting. The menu offers blood sausage, roast meats, and sauerkraut, all prepared using authentic recipes. Dining here feels like stepping into another era, making it a memorable experience.

2. Vanaema Juures (At Grandma's Place)

For a homestyle meal that echoes the warmth of a family Christmas dinner, Vanaema Juures is a must-visit. The restaurant is tucked away in the Old Town and serves traditional Estonian dishes like roast pork, sauerkraut, and potatoes, as if they were made by your Estonian grandmother. The portions are generous, and the flavors are comforting—perfect for a cozy evening.

3. Farm
Located near Town Hall Square, Farm focuses on modern Estonian cuisine while paying homage to the country's rural roots. During the Christmas season, they offer a special menu featuring seasonal dishes like blood sausage, sült, and traditional Estonian bread. The décor is warm and inviting, with rustic touches that nod to Estonia's countryside.

4. Rataskaevu 16
This popular restaurant is known for its seasonal ingredients and soulful dishes. During the Christmas season, expect to find a mix of traditional and modern Estonian dishes, such as roast pork with cranberry sauce and hearty servings of sauerkraut. The intimate, warm setting makes it a great choice for couples or small groups looking to enjoy a festive meal.

5. Leib Resto ja Aed
For a more contemporary take on traditional Estonian cuisine, Leib Resto ja Aed offers farm-to-table dishes with a Christmas twist. Their chefs focus on local, sustainable ingredients, and during the holiday season,

they highlight classic dishes like roast meats and Christmas bread, elevated with modern techniques.

A Food Lover's Christmas Market Tour

If you're a food lover, you're in for a real treat. Let's embark on a culinary adventure through the stalls, discovering local delicacies and seasonal street food that will make your taste buds sing.

Local Delicacies and Seasonal Street Food

As you approach the Town Hall Square, the first market that catches your eye will likely be bustling with excitement. Picture this: wooden stalls draped in twinkling fairy lights, each adorned with traditional decorations. You can almost hear the laughter and chatter of families and friends gathering to celebrate the holiday spirit.

Your journey begins at the food stalls, where the smell of verivorst (blood sausage) fills the air. This Estonian classic, made from pork and barley, is usually grilled to perfection. Don't be surprised if you find a crowd gathered around the vendor; locals swear by it. Grab a steaming plate topped with sauerkraut and a dollop of mustard—it's a hearty way to warm your soul on a chilly day.

Next, you can't miss out on kiluvõileib, a popular open-faced sandwich topped with sea herring, a staple in Estonian cuisine. Vendors often serve this delightful treat on a slice of dark rye bread, garnished with fresh herbs and a wedge of lemon. It's a refreshing burst of flavor that captures the essence of the sea.

As you continue your culinary exploration, look for stalls selling mulgipuder—a comforting potato and groat porridge. This traditional dish embodies the heartiness of Estonian winter food. Often served with a generous helping of melted butter, it's the perfect antidote to the cold, inviting you to linger and savor each bite.

And let's not forget about sweets! Your taste buds will dance with delight at the sight of piparkoogid, traditional gingerbread cookies that come in various shapes, often decorated with colorful icing. They're not just a treat for your taste buds but also a feast for the eyes. Try one with your coffee or hot cocoa, and you'll feel the warmth of Christmas enveloping you.

If you're feeling adventurous, look for kama, a unique blend of ground grains, often mixed with yogurt or milk. This ancient Estonian dish offers a slightly nutty flavor that might surprise you, especially when paired with a drizzle of honey or fresh berries. It's not just food; it's a taste of history, connecting you to Estonian culture with each spoonful.

Cozy Cafés and Bakeries

After indulging in savory bites, you'll want to warm up with a cozy drink. As the snowflakes begin to fall, the local cafés attract you with their inviting atmosphere. Café Maiasmokk, the oldest café in Tallinn, is a delightful stop. The moment you step inside, you'll immediately smell the aroma of freshly baked pastries wrapped around you and see many people already having a nice time.

Don't miss trying their karask, a traditional Estonian barley bread. It's dense and hearty, perfect when slathered with butter. Pair it with a steaming cup of kohvi (coffee) or a decadent hot chocolate topped with whipped cream, and you'll feel the chill of winter melt away.

Next, venture over to Rukis, a modern bakery that prides itself on using local ingredients. Their punsch—a spiced warm drink made with rum, tea, and fruit—will ignite your holiday spirit. It's not just a drink; it's a festive hug in a mug. As you sip, take a moment to admire the intricate pastries displayed in the glass case, including cinnamon rolls that practically sing to you with their sweet, spicy aroma.

For something sweeter, look for the bakery's strudel, filled with seasonal fruits and a hint of cinnamon. Each bite reveals layers of flaky goodness, warming you from the inside out. Grab a seat by the window and watch the world go by as you savor every morsel.

If you have a sweet tooth that craves something extra special, head over to Kohvik Komeet. This café is renowned for its Estonian cream cake—a delightful blend of cream, sponge cake, and berries. It's a dessert that speaks to the heart of Estonian festive traditions. The layers of cream are so light that you'll find yourself reaching for another slice before you even realize it.

As the day unfolds, don't hesitate to explore other cozy nooks around the Old Town. Each café has its own personality, from rustic charm to contemporary elegance. Stop by Café euphoria for a unique twist on hot beverages, like their chai latte infused with local spices. You might even stumble upon live music or local art exhibitions that will enrich your experience.

The Unforgettable Flavor of Tallinn's Christmas Markets

The true beauty of Tallinn's Christmas markets lies not only in the delightful array of food and drinks but also in the communal spirit they foster. People from all walks of life come together to share laughter, stories, and culinary experiences. Each bite and sip tells a story, weaving together threads of tradition and innovation, reminding you that food has the power to connect us all.

As the sun sets and the city glows in the warm light of the market stalls, you'll find yourself embracing the festive ambiance. Whether it's your first time or a cherished tradition, Tallinn's Christmas markets offer a feast that's as much about the flavors as it is about the memories you create.

So grab a friend or meet fellow travelers, and let the spirit of the season guide you through Tallinn's festive culinary journey. With every bite, you'll uncover the essence of Estonia, creating delicious memories that will linger long after your visit. Here's to savoring the season and indulging in the sweet and savory delights of Tallinn's Christmas market tour.

Chapter Five

Holiday Events and Festivities

Major Events and Festivals

The holiday season in Tallinn isn't just about twinkling lights and beautifully decorated trees; it's a celebration that resonates deeply within the hearts of the locals. In 2024, Tallinn offers a delightful array of events and festivals that will leave you with unforgettable memories. Let's explore the exciting holiday calendar and dive into the captivating world of Christmas carols and concerts in the city's historic churches.

Festive Events to Mark on Your Calendar

Every year is always wonderful and different from the previous with each corner revealing a new festive surprise. There are a lot of activities to do in Tallinn during Christmas. Here are some must-visit events and festivals you won't want to miss:

1. Tallinn Christmas Market (November 24, 2024 - January 7, 2025)

This is where it all begins! The Tallinn Christmas Market opens its doors at the Town Hall Square, transforming the area into a winter wonderland. Here, you'll find charming stalls brimming with handcrafted goods, traditional foods, and delightful beverages. Sip on steaming mulled wine while savoring a warm gingerbread cookie, and don't forget to take home a unique gift or two. This market is not just for shopping; it's an experience that fills your senses with holiday cheer.

2. Christmas Eve Celebrations (December 24, 2024)

On Christmas Eve, the city becomes a hub of festivities. Many locals gather with family for traditional feasts, but visitors are also welcomed to partake in the celebrations. Enjoy the beautiful decorations throughout the city, and you might catch a glimpse of the festive lights reflecting off the snow, creating a picturesque scene.

3. New Year's Eve Fireworks (December 31, 2024)

As the year wraps up, join the locals in welcoming the new year with a bang! Gather at the Freedom Square or Tallinn's Old Town to witness stunning fireworks lighting up the night sky. It's a joyous way to embrace the fresh start that awaits.

4. Tallinn Winter Festival (January 2025)

Once Christmas is over, the festive spirit doesn't fade; it simply transforms. The Tallinn Winter Festival showcases winter sports, outdoor activities, and cultural performances throughout January. Enjoy ice skating, snowshoeing, and perhaps even a thrilling dog sledding experience as you embrace the beautiful Estonian winter.

Christmas Carols and Concerts

One of the most captivating aspects of Tallinn's holiday celebrations is its rich musical heritage. Historic churches throughout the city open their doors for concerts and carol singing, allowing you to immerse yourself in the heart of Estonian traditions. Here's a closer look at what you can expect from the musical offerings this holiday season.

1. Concerts at St. Mary's Cathedral

Nestled in the heart of Tallinn's Old Town, St. Mary's Cathedral, also known as Toomkirik, is a magnificent venue for Christmas concerts. With its stunning medieval architecture and exquisite acoustics, the cathedral hosts various performances throughout December. Local choirs often gather here to sing traditional carols, filling the space with harmonious melodies that echo through the ancient stone walls. Attending a concert here isn't just a musical experience; it's a journey back in time, where you can feel the history of the city blend seamlessly with the spirit of Christmas.

2. The Estonian National Opera

If you're looking for a more elaborate musical experience, the Estonian National Opera presents a series of holiday-themed performances in December. Enjoy enchanting operatic renditions of classic Christmas carols, as well as festive ballets that tell timeless stories through dance. The opera house itself is a stunning sight, and the performances promise to be an extraordinary highlight of your holiday experience.

3. Caroling in the Streets

Beyond formal concerts, you'll find spontaneous caroling in the streets and squares of Tallinn. Join locals as they gather to sing beloved holiday songs. Whether it's a simple gathering near a Christmas tree or a larger performance in a public square, the atmosphere is warm and inviting. Don't be shy—jump in, and maybe even learn a few Estonian carols along the way!

4. Christmas Organ Concerts

For a truly unique musical experience, attend an organ concert at St. Nicholas Church. Known for its remarkable organ and historical significance, the church hosts special Christmas organ concerts featuring both classic and contemporary compositions. The deep, resonant sounds of the organ, paired with the candlelit ambiance of the church, create a mesmerizing setting that will leave you spellbound.

Joining in the Festivities

While attending concerts and events, don't hesitate to engage with the locals. Estonians are known for their warm hospitality, and you'll often find them eager to share their traditions with visitors. Ask about their favorite holiday songs or join in a festive toast at a local pub after a concert.

Consider planning your itinerary to allow for spontaneous moments. Some of the best experiences come from wandering through the snowy streets, discovering hidden musical performances, or stumbling upon impromptu holiday gatherings.

The blend of history, culture, and festive cheer creates an atmosphere that is truly one-of-a-kind. So grab your warmest coat, lace up those boots, and get ready to sing along as you uncover the joys of Christmas in Tallinn.

Tallinn's Christmas Parade

As the festive season envelops Tallinn in its winter embrace, one of the city's most delightful traditions comes alive: the Christmas Parade. Picture this: a snowy backdrop as the streets come alive with color, sound, and joyful cheer. This annual event typically takes place in early December, marking the official start of the holiday season in the city.

Families gather, their faces lit with anticipation, children bundled up in scarves and mittens, eyes wide with excitement. The atmosphere is electric, a sense of community filling the air. The parade winds through the cobbled streets of the Old Town, starting from the Town Hall Square and making its way through the historic center. Along the route, spectators line the sidewalks, eager to catch a glimpse of the festive floats and performers that pass by.

Local schools, community groups, and cultural organizations take part in this lively procession, each bringing their unique flair to the festivities. Expect to see colorful floats adorned with lights, twinkling like stars against the darkening sky. Dancers clad in traditional costumes sway gracefully, while musicians fill the air with cheerful melodies.

But the real heart of the parade lies in its spirit. Each year, a different theme is chosen, reflecting the traditions and culture of Estonia.

From folklore to contemporary interpretations, the parade tells stories that resonate with both locals and visitors. Make sure to check the schedule ahead of time to find out the exact date and theme for 2024; it's a highlight you won't want to miss!

After the parade, the excitement continues as the festive lights twinkle overhead. Grab a warm cup of glögi (Estonian mulled wine) and wander over to the Christmas market, where you can enjoy local treats and shop for handmade crafts. The parade is more than just a display; it's a communal experience, a gathering that reminds us of the joys of the season.

Ice Skating in Old Town

If you're in Tallinn during the winter months, ice skating in the Old Town is an absolute activity to do. Imagine gliding over smooth, glistening ice surrounded by medieval buildings adorned with festive decorations. The main ice rink is located right in the heart of the Town Hall Square, making it a perfect spot to experience the holiday skating scene.

The rink typically opens in late November, offering a picturesque setting for both seasoned skaters and those trying it for the first time. Rentals are available nearby, so no need to pack your own skates—just slip on a pair and hit the ice!

As you skate, take a moment to admire your surroundings. The Town Hall, with its imposing tower, stands sentinel over the square, and the sound of laughter fills the air. If you need a break from skating, the cozy kiosks nearby serve hot drinks and snacks. Treat yourself to some freshly baked gingerbread or a warm pretzel; after all, nothing warms you up like a little indulgence after some winter fun!

Ice skating in Tallinn isn't just about the activity; it's an experience that captures the essence of winter joy by meeting new people. If you're lucky, you might even catch a local ice dance performance or a spontaneous holiday-themed event on the rink. The atmosphere is friendly and inviting, making it a great spot for families, friends, and couples alike. Whether you glide gracefully or wobble with laughter, you're sure to create memories that will last a lifetime.

For the best experience, try to visit during the evening when the rink is illuminated by twinkling lights. The combination of laughter, music, and the aroma of holiday treats creates an atmosphere that feels like stepping into a festive postcard. Don't forget to take photos to capture the moment.

Special Seasonal Events

Beyond the parade and ice skating, Tallinn offers a plethora of seasonal events that showcase the city's cultural richness. Throughout December, various museums and galleries host special exhibits, workshops, and art shows that reflect the festive spirit and Estonia's artistic heritage.

The Estonian National Museum, for instance, often features exhibitions that delve into the history of Estonian Christmas traditions. You'll find displays of traditional crafts, ornaments, and photographs that tell the story of how Estonians have celebrated the season over the years. Guided tours are usually available, providing insightful commentary that enriches your understanding of the exhibits.

If you're feeling creative, why not participate in a workshop? Many local artisans offer classes where you can learn the art of creating traditional Christmas decorations or making your own gingerbread cookies. These workshops are not only fun but also provide a unique opportunity to connect with locals and fellow travelers, all while immersing yourself in the holiday spirit.

Art shows pop up in various galleries, showcasing the works of both established and emerging artists. These exhibitions often have a holiday theme, making it a wonderful chance to pick up unique gifts or simply enjoy the talent on display. Keep an eye out for pop-up markets featuring local artisans, where you can find one-of-a-kind pieces that truly embody the spirit of Estonian craftsmanship.

Another seasonal highlight is the Tallinn Christmas market's special events. Throughout the month, various performances take place, ranging from live music to theatrical productions. Local choirs often perform traditional Christmas carols, creating a melodious backdrop as you explore the market stalls.

Whether you're a culture enthusiast or just looking for something fun to do, Tallinn's seasonal events offer a bit of everything. From exhibits to workshops and performances, there's no shortage of ways to immerse yourself in the festive atmosphere.

You'll at the end discover that each event has its own story to tell, adding depth to your journey. The spirit of Christmas in Tallinn is alive in every corner, from the laughter of children in the streets to the warmth of the local community coming together to celebrate.

Chapter Six

A Family Christmas in Tallinn

When you think of family travel during the Christmas season, the first image that often comes to mind is the joy in a child's eyes as they explore new sights and experiences with you. Tallinn, with its enchanting blend of history and festive spirit, is a wonderful place for families to create unforgettable memories. Let's dive into some delightful child-friendly attractions and activities that will have your little ones squealing with joy.

Child-Friendly Attractions and Activities

1. Tallinn Zoo
One of the highlights for families visiting Tallinn is the Tallinn Zoo. Located on the outskirts of the city, this is a fantastic place to spend a day with your kids. The zoo is home to over 350 species, including the famous Estonian brown bear, reindeer, and even some exotic animals like tigers and penguins. The

open-air exhibits are perfect for letting kids roam free while learning about the animals. During winter, the zoo organizes special events, like "Winter Wonderland" days, where you can see how animals adapt to the chilly weather.

2. Seaplane Harbour (Lennusadam)
Step into a world of maritime adventure at the Seaplane Harbour. This interactive museum, housed in a historic seaplane hangar, is an absolute hit among families. Kids can climb aboard submarines, explore a replica of an icebreaker, and even try their hand at navigating a virtual boat. The massive aquarium also showcases Estonia's underwater life, making it both educational and entertaining. Special holiday-themed activities are often organized here, so check their schedule for fun events while you're in town.

Tallinn Christmas Market

While it's a must-see for everyone, the Tallinn Christmas Market is particularly delightful for families. The market, located in the heart of the Old Town, is bustling with cheerful activity, including a carousel that is sure to bring smiles to young faces. Children can indulge in sweet treats like gingerbread cookies and warm up with hot chocolate. Plus, the market often features activities like puppet shows and storytelling sessions that capture the imagination of little ones.

4. Estonian Maritime Museum
Another gem that kids love is the Estonian Maritime Museum. Located in the historic Fat Margaret tower, this museum offers a hands-on experience where children can engage with maritime history. From navigating an actual ship's wheel to learning about the seas, there's plenty to explore. The museum's special exhibits around Christmas often include festive decorations and themed activities.

Visiting the Estonian Open Air Museum's Christmas Village

No family trip to Tallinn during the holiday season would be complete without a visit to the Estonian Open Air Museum. It is located in a beautiful wooded area on the outskirts of the city. This open-air museum offers a fascinating glimpse into Estonia's rural life throughout history.

The museum features charmingly restored buildings from different eras, including farmhouses, windmills, and a village school. During Christmas, the museum transforms into a winter wonderland, and it's a spectacular sight to behold.

Kids can participate in traditional Estonian Christmas activities, like crafting ornaments and making gingerbread cookies, alongside local artisans. They might also get to meet Santa Claus, who often visits during the holiday season, bringing cheer and laughter to children of all ages.

The Christmas Village at the Open Air Museum captures the essence of how Estonians celebrate this special season. Visitors can enjoy live music, traditional folk dances, and seasonal food that the whole family can enjoy. Imagine biting into a warm, freshly baked cinnamon roll while your children watch an exciting puppet show.

One of the most charming aspects of the museum is how it immerses families in the cultural traditions of Estonia. Your kids can learn about old customs, such as how families used to celebrate Christmas with songs, dances, and storytelling. The atmosphere is warm and inviting, making it easy for everyone to feel at home in this historical setting.

After a day filled with activities, the whole family can take a leisurely stroll along the scenic pathways, enjoying the beauty of snow-covered landscapes. The museum's surrounding forests offer a peaceful retreat, perfect for unwinding after the excitement of the day.

Fun on Ice

For families, this is the perfect opportunity to dive into some thrilling winter activities that will leave your kids with beaming smiles and unforgettable memories.

Ice Skating

One of the most delightful winter pastimes in Tallinn is ice skating. The city boasts several outdoor rinks that come alive when the temperatures drop. The most popular spot is the outdoor rink in Town Hall Square, right in the heart of the Old Town. Imagine gliding under the soft glow of fairy lights, surrounded by medieval architecture. It's not just about skating; it's a whole experience!

If you're worried about your little ones taking their first steps on ice, don't fret! The rink offers skating aids shaped like penguins that your kids can hold onto for support. Rentals are available on-site, so no need to haul your gear around. After a fun session on the ice, warm up with a cup of hot cocoa from one of the nearby stalls—perfect for sipping while watching the world go by.

For more experienced skaters, head over to Jaan Poska Park, which features a larger rink often filled with families enjoying their time together. Here, kids can challenge their friends or parents to a friendly race, and there's plenty of space for a bit of fun-filled frolicking.

Sledding

Now, let's not forget about sledding. Tallinn parks transform into natural playgrounds, ideal for thrilling sledding adventures. Kumu Art Museum is a fantastic place for this; its nearby hill is perfect for kids (and adults) to zoom down on sleds, laughter echoing through the air. Just grab a sled from one of the local shops or rental places, and you're all set for a day filled with exhilarating rides.

Another great spot is Kadriorg Park. The undulating hills here provide just the right slopes for an exciting sledding experience. Afterward, you can take a stroll through the park's beautiful gardens, which look stunning under a soft layer of snow.

Holiday Parks and Family Entertainment

As the holiday spirit fills the air, Tallinn's family-friendly attractions kick into high gear. There's an abundance of parks and entertainment options that cater specifically to children, ensuring they have a blast during your visit.

Tallinna Loomaaed (Tallinn Zoo)

A visit to Tallinna Loomaaed, or Tallinn Zoo, is an excellent way to blend education with fun. While some animals may be more active than others in the cold, the zoo offers unique indoor exhibits, including an impressive tropical house. Kids can explore the wonders of nature while learning about different species. The zoo's layout is kid-friendly, allowing for easy navigation as they dash from one exhibit to another.

During the winter months, the zoo often hosts holiday-themed activities, where kids can engage with animals through special feeding sessions or crafting winter-themed decorations for their habitats. Check their schedule before your visit, as these activities can vary.

Christmas Village at Tallinna Raekoja Plats (Town Hall Square)

Another must-visit destination is the Christmas Village set up in Town Hall Square. While the main focus is the charming market, various attractions cater to children. Think carousel rides, mini-golf, and sometimes even ice sculpting demonstrations! Your kids will be captivated by the colorful stalls brimming with toys, treats, and holiday goodies.

For families seeking a more playful atmosphere, the Puppet Theatre often hosts performances in the square, showcasing beloved tales that engage young audiences. These lively shows usually include interactive elements that invite kids to participate, making them a fun way to immerse themselves in the holiday spirit.

Storytelling Sessions, Puppet Shows, and Interactive Christmas Workshops for Kids

One of the most delightful ways to introduce your children to Tallinn's holiday culture is through storytelling sessions and puppet shows that capture the essence of the season.

Storytelling Sessions

During the holiday season, libraries and community centers across Tallinn often organize storytelling sessions that breathe life into Estonian folklore and Christmas traditions. These events are usually held in cozy, intimate settings where children can sit on the floor, eagerly listening to enchanting tales told by engaging narrators. This is not just about hearing stories; it's a chance for children to ask questions and interact, creating a rich learning experience.

You'll find that many sessions encourage kids to share their own stories or to create a narrative of their own, guided by the storyteller's prompts. It's an excellent opportunity for little ones to let their imaginations soar while building confidence in expressing themselves.

Puppet Shows

Tucked away in various corners of the city, puppet theaters spring to life during the holiday season. The Tallinn Puppet Theatre is a fantastic place to catch a show. With colorful puppets and whimsical sets, these performances often blend classic tales with a festive twist, leaving children (and adults) chuckling and captivated.

The atmosphere in the theater is always lively, with children encouraged to cheer for their favorite characters or even interact with the puppets. Some performances may feature holiday-themed stories that emphasize the importance of kindness, friendship, and the joy of giving.

Interactive Christmas Workshops

Additionally, interactive workshops pop up throughout Tallinn in December, allowing children to create their own holiday crafts. From making Christmas ornaments to decorating gingerbread cookies, these workshops are led by local artisans and are designed to inspire creativity.

Check out places like Tallinn Creative Hub, which often host seasonal workshops specifically aimed at families. These hands-on experiences allow kids to dive into the crafting world, take home their creations, and share their newfound skills with family and friends.

Chapter Seven

Winter Adventures Outside the City

A Day Trip to Lahemaa National Park

As the snow blankets the landscape, there's something undeniably enchanting about Lahemaa National Park in winter. Just a short drive from Tallinn, this stunning natural reserve transforms into a winter wonderland that beckons outdoor enthusiasts and nature lovers alike. So grab your snowshoes, bundle up, and get ready for a day filled with adventure and discovery.

Imagine waking up early, the crisp air filling your lungs as you set out on the journey from Tallinn. The drive to Lahemaa takes about an hour, weaving through picturesque countryside that looks like it's straight out of a postcard. As you approach the park, the trees stand tall and proud, their branches heavy with snow, creating a serene atmosphere that instantly sets the stage for your winter escapade.

Once you arrive at Lahemaa, you're greeted by a world where silence reigns, interrupted only by the crunch of snow beneath your feet. This is where snowshoeing becomes a thrilling exploration. You don't need to be an expert; the gentle trails are suitable for everyone, allowing you to trek through the forest at your own pace. Picture yourself surrounded by towering pines, their needles glistening under a fresh layer of snow, while the soft sunlight filters through the branches. It's like stepping into a scene from a winter fairy tale.

Lahemaa is home to various animals, including moose, deer, and even the elusive lynx. While they might be harder to spot during the colder months, their tracks can often lead you to fascinating stories of their daily lives. With a little patience and a keen eye, you might just catch a glimpse of these majestic creatures or their footprints leading into the underbrush.

For those who want a deeper understanding of the park's ecosystem, consider joining a guided snowshoeing tour. Knowledgeable guides share insights about the flora and fauna, along with local legends that add a layer of intrigue to your adventure. They'll point out trees that have stood for centuries and share stories about the rich cultural history of the area, making your experience all the more engaging.

After a morning filled with snowshoeing, it's time to warm up and recharge. Pack a thermos of hot chocolate or find a cozy spot in one of the nearby visitor centers, where you can enjoy a warm meal while looking out over the snowy landscape. The combination of fresh air and a hearty lunch will leave you feeling invigorated, ready for the next adventure.

Skiing and Snowboarding

If snowshoeing isn't your style, fear not—Tallinn boasts fantastic options for skiing and snowboarding, providing thrilling experiences for both beginners and seasoned pros.

One of the most popular spots is Kurtna, located about 30 kilometers from Tallinn. This ski resort is known for its well-groomed slopes and a friendly atmosphere. Whether you're strapping on a snowboard for the first time or looking to refine your skills, Kurtna has something for everyone. The slopes are manageable, making it perfect for families or those just starting their winter sports journey.

After a day on the slopes, you can unwind in the lodge with a warm drink or a hearty meal. The atmosphere here is relaxed, with fellow skiers sharing stories of their day on the snow.

Another great option is Nõmme Ski Center, which is closer to the city and offers a more urban experience. It features illuminated slopes for evening skiing, allowing you to enjoy the thrill of gliding down under the stars. Rentals are easily available, so you don't need to bring your own gear. Plus, the vibrant atmosphere makes it a fun place to meet fellow snow enthusiasts.

For a unique experience, consider Oru, which offers a combination of skiing, snowboarding, and cross-country trails. Here, the scenery changes as you glide through the serene forests, surrounded by nature's beauty. The varied terrain caters to all skill levels, ensuring everyone can find their perfect slope.

Is it either you choose the tranquil snowshoeing trails of Lahemaa National Park or the lively slopes of Tallinn's ski resorts. Your winter adventure in Estonia promises to be filled with excitement, discovery, and unforgettable memories.

Explore the Beaches

As you stroll along the coast of Tallinn, winter paints a unique scene, transforming the landscape into a wintry masterpiece. The once-bustling beaches take on a new identity under a blanket of snow and ice, inviting you to explore their quiet beauty.

First on your list should be Pirita Beach, a local favorite. During the summer, it's filled with sunbathers and families enjoying the warm weather, but in winter, it's eerily serene. Walk along the shoreline, where the waves gently lap against the ice-encased rocks. You might even catch glimpses of local photographers capturing the stark beauty of the landscape. Keep an eye out for the Tallinn Lighthouse, also known as the Pirita Lighthouse. Standing tall against the backdrop of a winter sky, it has been guiding sailors since the 19th century. You can't enter the lighthouse in winter, but a photo stop is a must—it's particularly striking when the sun sets, casting a soft glow over the frozen waters.

Next, venture a bit further to Kakumäe Beach, known for its beautiful wooden piers and tranquil atmosphere. Here, you can stroll along the coast, with the icy Baltic Sea to your left and a forested area to your right. If you're lucky, you might spot ice skaters gliding gracefully on nearby frozen ponds. The silence here is captivating, allowing you to connect with nature in a way that's often lost amid the city's hustle.

If you feel adventurous, consider a guided ice fishing experience. Local fishermen often lead tours where you can drill a hole in the ice and try your luck at catching some fish. Not only is it a unique activity, but it also immerses you in the local culture, as you learn about the techniques and traditions passed down through generations.

Tallinn's Nature Trails

The city's surrounding nature trails offer an enchanting escape from urban life. Grab your hiking boots and prepare for a day of adventure surrounded by snow-laden trees and peaceful landscapes.

One of the most popular trails is located within Tallinn's Kadriorg Park, which is a winter wonderland in its own right. The park's historic paths wind through the stunning gardens, now blanketed in white, with frozen ponds adding to the scenery. As you walk, you'll pass by the Kadriorg Palace, an exquisite baroque structure that looks magnificent against the winter backdrop. Bring your camera; every turn offers a new perspective of this lovely park, especially with the palace reflecting the soft winter light.

If you're looking for a more immersive experience, head over to Tallinna Loodusmuuseum (Tallinn Nature Museum). From here, you can access several hiking routes that lead into the nearby forests. These trails offer a chance to see the local wildlife, such as deer or even the occasional fox. The paths are well-marked, so you don't need to worry about getting lost. Just make sure you're bundled up, as the forests can feel quite chilly when the wind picks up.

For those seeking a more challenging hike, consider the Aegviidu Nature Trail. Located a short drive from Tallinn, this trail stretches through the Estonian wilderness. You'll encounter towering pines and frozen marshlands, with opportunities to observe local fauna. The fresh air, combined with the peaceful sounds of nature, creates a sense of rejuvenation that is hard to describe. It's a chance to disconnect from the fast-paced world and connect with the tranquility of winter.

Don't forget to pack a thermos filled with hot cocoa or tea! There's nothing quite like taking a break along the trail, surrounded by nature, with the warmth of a cozy drink in hand. Embrace the silence and solitude of the woods; it's a perfect moment to reflect and appreciate the beauty of winter in Tallinn.

Adventure Tours

After your peaceful forest adventures, it's time to kick the adrenaline up a notch! Winter in Tallinn is not just about the scenery; it's also about experiencing the thrill of unique activities that embrace the cold weather. One of the highlights is husky sledding, where you can embark on a thrilling ride through the snowy landscapes.

Several local tour operators offer husky sledding experiences, usually located just outside of Tallinn. Imagine being pulled by a team of enthusiastic, furry huskies as they race across the snow. You'll be guided by an expert musher who will teach you the basics of sled handling. The rush of the wind against your face and the joyful barks of the dogs will make you feel alive. It's an adventure that captures the spirit of winter in Estonia, and the dogs are simply delightful.

After an exhilarating ride, take a moment to bond with the dogs. They are incredibly friendly and love the attention, making this a memorable experience for animal lovers. You might even get a chance to help harness them before the sledding begins—definitely a highlight of the day!

If you prefer a more relaxed pace, consider booking a horse-drawn sleigh ride. Imagine gliding silently through the snow-covered forests, wrapped in warm blankets, as the horses trot along the path. It's a beautiful way to appreciate the wintry landscape and a perfect activity for families or couples looking for a romantic outing. Many tours include stops for hot drinks by a cozy campfire, where you can share stories and enjoy the peacefulness of nature.

You can find sleigh rides offered near Tallinn and in nearby areas, such as Viimsi or Lahemaa National Park. These tours often have knowledgeable guides who share fascinating tales about the region's history, wildlife, and traditions, making the experience both entertaining and informative.

Chapter Eight

Estonia's Unique Christmas Traditions

Christmas Eve Sauna

For Estonians, the sauna symbolizes cleansing—not just physically, but spiritually. On Christmas Eve, families start the day by meticulously preparing their sauna, cleaning it, and ensuring it's ready for the ceremonial sweat. The air fills with the soothing scent of birch leaves and the warmth radiates from the stones heated to perfection. This is where the magic of connection happens.

Before moving in, it's customary to make a wish or reflect on the past year. As you slip into the steamy embrace of the sauna, the world outside fades away, leaving behind the hustle and bustle of holiday preparations. You can hear the gentle whispers of stories being shared, laughter echoing off the wooden walls, and the crackling of birch leaves as they're gently slapped against the skin—a traditional practice believed to improve circulation and rejuvenate the body.

After the sauna session, a ritual plunge into cold water or a roll in the snow follows, invigorating the senses. This contrast is not just refreshing; it symbolizes rebirth and renewal. Once you're refreshed, it's time to return to the warmth of home. Families gather around the table, where a feast awaits, full of traditional dishes like sauerkraut, roast pork, and gingerbread cookies—each bite a testament to the flavors of the season.

This Christmas Eve sauna ritual fosters a sense of community and connection. It's a moment to pause, reflect, and share hopes for the upcoming year. So, if you find yourself in Tallinn during this festive season, don't miss the opportunity to partake in this heartwarming tradition.

Folklore and Legends

Estonia's long winter nights are perfect for storytelling, and the tales of mythical creatures and Christmas legends weave a rich narrative that captures the imagination. As the snow blankets the countryside, families gather around the fireplace, sharing these enchanting stories that have been passed down through generations.

One such character is Krampus, a mischievous creature who accompanies St. Nicholas. Unlike the jolly old man, Krampus is a horned figure, and legend has it that he punishes naughty children while rewarding the well-behaved. His antics are a reminder for kids to be good, especially during the holiday season. Imagine the excitement (and a little fear) in the air as children listen to the stories of Krampus's visits, hoping he'll overlook their minor mischief!

Then there's Kalevipoeg, the giant hero of Estonian folklore. His tales are often recounted during winter nights, as families immerse themselves in the epic adventures that shape their cultural identity. Kalevipoeg is not only a figure of strength but also embodies the spirit of resilience and bravery. His stories, filled with battles against dark forces and quests for justice, offer a sense of pride and connection to the land.

During Christmas, Estonians also celebrate Jõuluvana, the Estonian Santa Claus. Unlike the Western depiction, Jõuluvana has roots in ancient traditions. He's often portrayed as a wise old man who brings gifts to children. However, he also shares tales of the forest and the spirits that dwell within. These stories are a reminder of the deep connection between the people and their natural surroundings, and they serve to instill respect for the environment in the hearts of the young.

In addition to these tales, Christmas Eve is a time for more personal stories—memories of family gatherings, laughter, and shared meals. Each household has its own traditions that add flavor to the broader tapestry of Estonian Christmas folklore. The enchanting stories come alive in the warm glow of candlelight, where the echoes of laughter and the soft rustle of blankets create an atmosphere of coziness.

As you explore Tallinn during the holiday season, let the stories of Kalevipoeg, Krampus, and Jõuluvana guide your experience. Seek out local storytellers or visit cultural events where these tales are shared, bringing the essence of Estonian folklore to life. Engaging with these narratives will connect you with the heart and soul of its people. So, gather around the fire, listen closely, and allow the stories to transport you to a world where the past and present intertwine, creating an unforgettable holiday experience.

Holiday Superstitions and Customs

Try to stroll through Tallinn during the Christmas season. You'll discover intriguing superstitions that guide locals through this festive time. One of the most cherished traditions involves the lighting of candles. Families place candles in their windows to signify a warm welcome to travelers and a reminder to the spirits of loved ones who have passed. This simple act not only lights up the cold, dark nights but also carries a deep-rooted significance, symbolizing hope and remembrance.

Have you heard about the Estonian tradition of keeping a "Christmas pig"? This delightful custom is about more than just the feast. Families often prepare a small piglet made of dough, which they might place at the table as a token of prosperity and good fortune for the upcoming year. After the festivities, some families keep the pig until New Year's Eve, believing that it brings luck throughout the holidays.

When it comes to Santa Claus, Estonians have a unique twist. Known as Jõuluvana, or "Christmas Old Man," he's depicted as a jolly figure who visits homes to deliver gifts to children. Unlike the Western image of Santa, Jõuluvana often arrives in the company of a helper, who may be a little less jolly and more mischievous, ensuring children behave during the holiday season. This duo can often be seen at Christmas markets and community gatherings, adding to the festive atmosphere.

Understanding these customs can deepen your appreciation of the holiday season in Tallinn. As you explore the winding streets of the Old Town, look out for families carrying candles and perhaps even spot Jõuluvana making his rounds at the local markets. It's these traditions that give the holiday season its warmth and community spirit.

Traditional Songs and Dances

Music and dance are integral parts of Estonia's Christmas celebrations, reflecting the nation's rich cultural heritage. Imagine the sounds of traditional carols wafting through the air as you wander through the cobbled streets, surrounded by the sight of colorful decorations and the scent of mulled wine. It's a sensory experience that you won't want to miss.

One of the most beloved songs you might hear is "Jõulud" (Christmas), a festive tune that resonates with joy and nostalgia. The locals often gather in town squares and community centers to sing these traditional carols, inviting everyone—yes, even visitors—to join in. Don't be shy! Participating in these sing-alongs can be a wonderful way to connect with the local culture. If you're not familiar with the lyrics, simply enjoy the melodies and let the spirit of the season wash over you.

Dancing is another cherished tradition during Christmas in Tallinn. Folk dances such as the "Kaera-Jaani" and "Vana Jõuluvana" are often performed at various holiday events. You'll likely find groups of enthusiastic locals gathering around a bonfire or in community halls, eager to share these lively dances with anyone willing to participate. Learning a few simple steps can be a delightful way to bond with the community and make your trip memorable.

If you want to truly immerse yourself in the festive spirit, consider attending a Christmas concert or a local dance event. Many venues throughout the city host performances that celebrate both traditional and contemporary Estonian music. These events are a fantastic opportunity to witness the vibrancy of local culture and perhaps even meet some friendly faces along the way.

Local Christmas Crafts

There's something special about crafting your own holiday decorations, and in Tallinn, you'll find plenty of opportunities to dive into this creative endeavor. The spirit of the season is palpable in local workshops, where artisans share their skills and teach visitors the art of traditional Estonian crafts. From ornaments to wreaths, the options are endless, and each craft comes with its own story.

One popular craft during the holiday season is making "jõulutooted" or Christmas goods, often from natural materials like straw and wood. Picture yourself seated in a cozy workshop, surrounded by locals, as you learn to weave intricate patterns into straw ornaments that will adorn your Christmas tree. Not only are these decorations eco-friendly, but they also carry a piece of Estonian tradition that you can take home with you.

Another delightful craft is making festive wreaths. You'll find workshops that provide fresh pine, holly, and other natural materials, allowing you to create a beautiful centerpiece for your holiday table or a festive decoration for your door. As you craft your wreath, listen to the stories behind these traditions, learning about the significance of different plants and their ties to Estonian folklore.

For those with a flair for creativity, consider attending a pottery class where you can mold and paint your own holiday-themed ceramics. Imagine crafting a unique ornament or a charming dish that reflects your personal style while incorporating traditional designs. It's a wonderful way to connect with the local culture while creating lasting memories.

As you walk through Tallinn's markets, keep an eye out for stalls featuring handmade crafts from local artisans. Purchasing these items not only supports the community but also provides you with authentic souvenirs that carry the essence of your holiday experience.

Chapter Nine

Practical Tips During Christmas in Tallinn

Weather

Tallinn in December can be quite the contrast to the milder climates many travelers are accustomed to. Temperatures usually hover around -1°C to -5°C (30°F to 23°F), with the potential for colder spells as winter settles in. Snowfall is common, creating a picturesque winter landscape that feels like something out of a storybook.

Imagine walking through the cobbled streets of the Old Town, surrounded by medieval architecture dusted with white. The crisp air invigorates your senses, but it can bite if you're not prepared. To fully enjoy your exploration of Tallinn, layering is key. Start with a thermal base layer to keep your core warm, followed by a cozy sweater or fleece. On top, a good quality winter coat is essential; look for one that's insulated and waterproof to keep you dry during unexpected flurries.

Accessories play a significant role in your comfort. Don't underestimate the power of a warm hat—something that covers your ears will serve you well. A scarf is not just a fashion statement; it can be a lifesaver against biting winds. Opt for gloves that allow you to use your phone, as you'll want to capture the enchanting sights without freezing your fingers. Waterproof boots with good traction are a must if you plan to explore the charming but sometimes slippery streets of Tallinn. You'll appreciate them as you wander from market to market, sipping mulled wine and sampling gingerbread.

Budgeting Your Trip

While Tallinn offers a captivating experience during the Christmas season, it's wise to manage your budget to make the most of your trip without breaking the bank. First things first—let's talk about accommodations. Prices can vary greatly depending on where you stay and when you book. Popular hotels in the Old Town tend to fill up quickly as the holidays approach, so securing your lodging early can save you a chunk of change. Consider staying a little outside the main tourist areas; you can often find charming guest houses and apartments at more reasonable rates.

When it comes to dining, Tallinn is a delightful city for food lovers. You'll find everything from cozy cafés serving traditional Estonian dishes to gourmet restaurants. To keep your dining expenses in check, take advantage of lunch specials, which many places offer. This is a fantastic way to enjoy a hearty meal at a fraction of the dinner price. Street food is also a budget-friendly option, especially at Christmas markets. Indulging in local favorites like verivorst (blood sausage) or kama (a traditional grain mix) not only satisfies your hunger but also immerses you in Estonian culture.

Transportation is another factor to consider. Tallinn has an efficient public transport system that includes buses and trams. A single ticket costs around €2, but purchasing a Tallinn Card can be a smart investment. This card grants you unlimited travel on public transport and discounts at many attractions. Plus, the city's compact nature makes walking a pleasurable option, allowing you to soak in the sights while saving money.

Let's not forget about shopping! The Christmas markets are a treasure trove of handcrafted gifts and local delicacies. While it's easy to get carried away, set a budget for how much you'd like to spend on souvenirs. Prioritize items that are unique to Estonia, like traditional ornaments or locally made woolen goods. If you're eyeing a larger purchase, don't hesitate to ask the vendor if there's room for negotiation.

It's always good to have a buffer in your budget for unexpected expenses. Whether it's a spontaneous café stop or an impromptu visit to a museum, having a little extra set aside can help you embrace the experience without worrying too much about your finances.

By planning for the weather and keeping your expenses in check, you're setting yourself up for a wonderful adventure in Tallinn. You'll be able to focus on enjoying the festivities, discovering hidden gems, and creating unforgettable memories in this beautiful city during the Christmas season.

Public Transport Guide

God forbid but before you get lost in the allure of the Old Town, you'll need to figure out how to navigate the city like a local. Don't worry. This guide will walk you through Tallinn's public transport system, ensuring your journey is as smooth as the snowflakes falling from the sky. Whether you're hopping on a bus, gliding along in a tram, or catching a taxi, you'll find that getting around Tallinn is not only easy but can also be quite an adventure.

Understanding the Basics of Tallinn's Transport System

First things first: Tallinn boasts a well-organized public transport network comprising buses, trams, and trolleybuses. It's not just efficient; it's also friendly to the environment, which is a big plus for those who care about sustainability. The city uses a unified ticketing system, meaning you can use the same ticket for all forms of public transport. This makes hopping from one mode to another seamless—no need to fuss with different tickets!

One interesting aspect of Tallinn's public transport is that it is free for residents. Yes, you read that right! While you might not benefit from this perk, it's a testament to the city's commitment to keeping its residents connected. For visitors, purchasing a ticket is simple and affordable.

Buses: The Backbone of Urban Travel

Tallinn's buses are a reliable way to traverse the city and reach areas beyond the historic center. With more than 50 bus lines, they can take you to almost every nook and cranny of Tallinn. Most buses run frequently, especially during peak hours, so you won't have to wait long.

To catch a bus, just look for the stops marked with signs displaying the bus lines that serve that stop. The timetables are easy to read, displaying the times for each bus and the expected intervals. The red and yellow buses are pretty eye-catching too!

Buying Tickets: You can buy your tickets at ticket machines found at many bus stops or on board the bus (though it's slightly more expensive if you purchase on the bus). Consider getting a day pass if you plan to use the buses multiple times in a day. It gives you unlimited rides and can be a money-saver.

Tips for Using Buses

- Download the Tallinna Ühistranspordi app: It provides real-time schedules, maps, and even allows you to buy tickets directly on your phone.
- Mind the Rush Hours: Mornings and evenings can get busy, so try to plan your trips during off-peak times when you can enjoy a little more space.
- Listen for Announcements: Most buses have audio announcements that inform you of the next stop. Keep your ears open, especially if you're not yet familiar with the area!

Trams

Next up, let's talk about the trams. The tram network consists of four lines that connect various parts of the city, making them perfect for both tourists and locals. You'll often find the trams humming along their tracks, with the friendly faces of fellow travelers ready to share their experiences.

Tram Stops and Timetables: Tram stops are marked clearly, and the schedules are posted prominently. Like buses, trams operate frequently, so you won't find yourself waiting too long. The trams also have real-time displays showing when the next tram will arrive, which is super helpful.

Riding the Tram: One of the best things about tram rides is the view. You'll pass through beautiful neighborhoods, with architecture that tells the story of Tallinn's past. Grab a seat by the window, and enjoy the ride!

Tips for Using Trams

- Mind the Fare Zones: Make sure you're aware of which fare zone you're in to buy the correct ticket.
- Stay Aware: Some stops can be a bit crowded, especially during rush hour, so keep your belongings close.
- Connecting Lines: Many tram stops connect with bus lines, making it easy to switch modes of transport if needed.

Taxis

When the weather is biting and you're yearning for a warm ride, taxis in Tallinn can be a lifesaver. They're plentiful and can be found at taxi stands throughout the city or booked via various ride-hailing apps. While taxis aren't as cheap as public transport, they offer a comfortable way to reach your destination, especially late at night when other options may be limited.

Choosing a Taxi: Always look for licensed taxis that display a taxi sign on the roof. The meter should start running as soon as you enter the vehicle, and it's customary to round up the fare.

Popular Taxi Services: Some of the well-known taxi apps operating in Tallinn include Bolt and Uber. Download these apps to get quick rides, compare fares, and even pay through your phone—super convenient.

Tips for Using Taxis

- Plan Your Route: It can be helpful to have your destination address written down or saved on your phone to show the driver.

- Cash vs. Card: While most taxis accept cards, it's a good idea to have some cash handy, just in case.
- Ask for Recommendations: Don't hesitate to ask your driver for local tips or places to visit—they often have great insights!

Navigating with Ease

With this public transport guide in hand, you're all set to navigate Tallinn like a pro. Whether you choose the bus, tram, or a cozy taxi, you'll find that getting around this beautiful city is not just straightforward; it's part of the adventure. Each ride offers a glimpse into the life of Tallinn.

Bus Lines and How to Get There

When you arrive, you'll quickly realize that getting around this compact city is easier than you might think, especially with the extensive bus network at your disposal.

Understanding the Bus System

Tallinn's public transport system is well-organized and efficient, comprising buses, trams, and trolleys. However, for this adventure, we'll focus primarily on buses. The city operates a comprehensive network, connecting the city center to various neighborhoods, attractions, and even the outskirts. Whether you're heading to the historic Old Town, the bustling Telliskivi Creative City, or the picturesque Kadriorg Park, you'll find a bus line to get you there.

Buying Tickets

Before you hop on a bus, you'll need to secure your ticket. Tickets can be purchased at ticket machines located at major bus stops, convenience stores, or even via a mobile app. The beauty of Tallinn's system is the ease of use; you can choose between a single journey ticket or a day pass, which is great if you plan to explore multiple areas. Remember, once you buy your ticket, it's valid for a certain period, so make sure to keep an eye on the time if you opt for a single journey.

Popular Bus Lines

Now, let's talk about some key bus lines that will help you navigate the city seamlessly:

- Bus 2: This line is a favorite for tourists and locals alike, as it connects the airport to the city center. It's perfect if you're landing and want to dive straight into the sights without hassle. The bus takes you to major hubs like the Tallinn Bus Station and near the Old Town.

- Bus 3: If you're planning to visit the bustling Telliskivi Creative City, catch Bus 3. This trendy area is packed with cafes, galleries, and street art, making it a fantastic spot to spend a leisurely afternoon. The bus will drop you off just a short walk from the heart of the action.

- Bus 24: For those looking to soak up the history at the Estonian Open Air Museum or enjoy the lush surroundings of Kadriorg Park, Bus 24 is your go-to option. This route provides a scenic ride, letting you glimpse local life as you travel away from the more touristy areas.

- Bus 1: This route is perfect for reaching the Tallinn Zoo and the nearby entertainment area. If you're traveling with kids or just want to spend a fun day outdoors, this bus will take you right to your destination.

Timetables and Frequency

Buses generally run from early morning until midnight, with a frequency of about 10 to 20 minutes, depending on the time of day and route. Keep in mind that during peak hours, you might encounter a bit of a crowd, especially on popular lines. If you're unsure of when the next bus is coming, the real-time tracking information available at many stops will keep you updated.

Tips for a Smooth Ride

To make your bus journey as enjoyable as possible, consider these tips:

1. Plan Ahead: Check the bus schedules and routes in advance. The public transport app can be a lifesaver for this, showing you the best connections and travel times.

2. Mind Your Belongings: Like any bustling city, it's wise to keep an eye on your belongings while on the bus. Be aware of your surroundings, especially during busy times.

3. Enjoy the Ride: Take a moment to look out the window as you travel. Each bus ride offers a different perspective of the city, showcasing local life and charming neighborhoods you might not see otherwise.

Useful and Essential Estonian Phrases for Travelers

Traveling to Estonia is an exciting opportunity to immerse yourself in a culture that's unique and inviting. While many Estonians speak English, especially in urban areas like Tallinn, knowing a few phrases in the local language can enhance your experience and help you connect with locals. It's a way to show respect for their culture and can make your interactions more enjoyable. So, grab your notebook and jot down these essential Estonian phrases that will come in handy during your travels!

Greetings and Basic Phrases

1. Tere! (TEH-reh)
   Hello!
   A simple and friendly way to greet anyone you meet. You'll hear this often!

2. Head aega! (HEAD AH-eh-gah)
   Goodbye!
   Use this when you're leaving a place or saying farewell to someone.

3. Palun! (PAH-loon)
   Please!
   A polite way to ask for something or make a request.

4. Aitäh! (AEE-tah)
   Thank you!
   Use this phrase to express your gratitude when someone helps you.

5. Kuidas sul läheb? (KUID-as sool LEH-ehb?)
   How are you?
   A friendly way to ask someone about their well-being.

Essential Questions

6. Kus on...? (KOOS on...?)
   Where is...?
   Perfect for asking for directions. For example, "Kus on turg?" means "Where is the market?"

7. Kui palju see maksab? (KUI PAHL-yoo seh MAHK-sahb?)
   How much does this cost?
   Useful for shopping and dining, ensuring you're aware of prices.

8. Kas sa räägid inglise keelt? (KAS sah RAY-eeg-id IN-gli-seh KAYLT?)
   Do you speak English?
   A helpful phrase when you need to confirm if someone can communicate in English.

9. Vabandust! (VAH-band-ust)
   Excuse me!
   Use this to get someone's attention or to apologize if you accidentally bump into someone.

10. Miks? (MIKS?)
    Why?
    A simple yet essential word to understand reasoning or to inquire further during conversations.

Directions and Navigation

11. Paremale! (PAH-reh-mah-leh)
    To the right!
    A key phrase when following directions.

12. Vasakule! (VAH-sah-koo-leh)
   To the left!
   Use this to navigate your way around the city.

13. Otse! (OT-seh)
   Straight ahead!
   Perfect for when you need to continue on the same path.

14. Kaugel! (KOW-gel)
   Far away!
   This helps in understanding the distance to your destination.

15. Lähedal! (LEH-hah-dahl)
   Nearby!
   Great for finding places that are close by, like cafes or shops.

Dining and Shopping

16. Menüü palun! (MEH-noo-ee PAH-loon)
   Menu, please!
   Use this when dining at restaurants to ask for the menu.

17. Soovitaksin... (SOH-vee-tahk-sin...)
   I would recommend...

Handy when asking for suggestions on local dishes or drinks.

18. Vein või õlu? (VAYN VEE OOL-oo?)
   Wine or beer?
   A fun question to ask when choosing drinks.

19. Soodustus? (SOH-doo-stus?)
   Discount?
   Use this when shopping to inquire about any available deals.

20. Kas ma saaksin arve? (KAS mah SAHK-sin AR-veh?)
   Can I have the bill?
   This is essential when you're ready to pay after a meal.

Emergency and Assistance

21. Abi! (AH-bee!)
   Help!
   An important word to remember in case of emergencies.

22. Kus on haigla? (KOOS on HIH-gla?)
   Where is the hospital?
   Useful if you need medical assistance.

23. Ma olen kaotanud... (MAH OH-len KOW-tahn-ood...)

I have lost...

A phrase to use if you need help finding something you lost.

24. Helista politseisse! (HEH-lis-tah POL-ih-tseis-seh!)

Call the police!

Critical in an emergency situation.

25. Kas sa saad mind aidata? (KAS sah SAHD meend AID-ah-tah?)

Can you help me?

A direct way to ask someone for assistance.

Numbers

1. Üks
2. Kaks
3. Kolm
4. Neli
5. Viis
6. Kuus
7. Seitsme
8. Kaheksa
9. Üheksa
10. Kümme

These phrases are just the necessary component of your adventure in Estonia. While exploring Tallinn's cobblestone streets, remember that locals will appreciate your effort to speak their language. With these phrases in your back pocket, you'll feel more connected to the people and culture, making your journey all the more memorable.

Health and Safety Tips

With the right mindset and a few practical tips, you can enjoy all the festive wonders without shivering through your experiences. Let's dive into some essential health and safety tips to ensure you stay warm and safe.

Dress for the Occasion

First things first: layering is your best friend. Start with a moisture-wicking base layer to keep sweat away from your skin, followed by insulating layers like fleece or wool. A waterproof and windproof outer layer will protect you from the elements while allowing you to enjoy the stunning outdoor sights. Don't forget a good pair of thermal socks, gloves, a warm hat, and a scarf to wrap around your neck. Investing in quality winter boots with insulation and good grip will help you tackle icy sidewalks without slipping.

Hydrate and Nourish Yourself

While you might think of hydrating as something you do in the summer, it's just as important in winter. Cold air can be drying, and you might not feel thirsty as often, but keeping your body well-hydrated is crucial for maintaining warmth. Sip on hot beverages like herbal tea or mulled wine while exploring the Christmas adventures.

Remember to nourish your body with hearty meals. Traditional Estonian dishes often feature warming ingredients like potatoes, root vegetables, and meats, perfect for fueling your winter adventures. Try to sit down for a meal at one of Tallinn's cozy restaurants, where you can enjoy a local dish while warming up from the inside out.

Know the Local Health Services

Familiarize yourself with local health services before your trip. Tallinn boasts well-equipped hospitals and clinics, and it's good to know where to go in case of an emergency. Consider purchasing travel insurance that covers medical expenses—this way, you can explore without worries. Keep a small first aid kit with you for minor issues like cuts or scrapes, especially if you're venturing into nature.

Safety in the City

Tallinn is generally safe, but like any tourist destination, it's wise to remain vigilant. Stay aware of your surroundings, especially in crowded places like Christmas markets where pickpockets might be lurking. Use a secure bag that you can keep close to your body, and avoid displaying valuable items like expensive cameras or jewelry.

As you explore the Old Town's cobblestone streets, be cautious of slippery patches, especially when they're covered in snow or ice. Take your time and wear appropriate footwear to avoid accidents. If you're enjoying a drink at one of the festive bars, know your limits. The local drinks can be quite potent, and it's essential to stay alert while navigating the city after dark.

Embrace the Estonian Winter

Tallinn offers a range of outdoor activities that can keep you moving and warm, such as ice skating at the Town Hall Square or taking a scenic walk through Kadriorg Park. Dress warmly and shabby. Engaging in physical activity will help you stay warm and provide a different perspective on the city.

Emergency Contacts and What to

When traveling, especially during the peak holiday season in a new place like Tallinn, it's important to be prepared for emergencies. Unforeseen circumstances can happen, and knowing what to do can save time and keep stress to a minimum. Here's everything you need to know about emergency contacts and what to do if you encounter a tricky situation while enjoying your time in Tallinn.

Who to Call: Key Emergency Numbers

Tallinn has a reliable and efficient emergency system, so if something goes wrong, you're in good hands. Estonia uses the universal emergency number 112, which connects you to all major services. Whether you need the police, medical assistance, or fire services, dialing 112 is your go-to solution. Operators speak Estonian, but they are also fluent in English and Russian, making communication easy for international travelers.

If you happen to lose your phone, there are public phones available in parts of the city, and many businesses will let you use their phone in an emergency. Locals are generally helpful and will assist if you ask them to contact emergency services for you.

Dealing with Health Emergencies

Let's say you're walking through Town Hall Square, enjoying some mulled wine, and suddenly feel unwell. Don't panic! Tallinn has excellent healthcare facilities. If you need an ambulance, call 112, and emergency medical services will arrive promptly. The paramedics are well-trained and experienced in dealing with a wide range of situations.

For non-urgent medical assistance, you can visit one of the local hospitals or clinics. North Estonia Medical Centre is a reliable choice, and they have services available for tourists. Make sure you have travel insurance, as it helps cover the cost of any treatments. Pharmacies are also easy to find and are stocked with over-the-counter medications for minor issues like colds or stomach aches. Ask for an apteek, which is the Estonian word for pharmacy.

Lost or Stolen Belongings

Losing your wallet or phone is frustrating, especially when you're far from home. In the case of theft or lost items, the first step is to file a report with the local police. Visit the nearest police station or dial 112 to inform them. Keep copies of important documents, like your passport and travel insurance details, stored digitally or in a separate location from the originals. If you lose your passport, head to your country's nearest embassy or consulate in Tallinn for assistance. They will help you with the paperwork needed to get a temporary travel document.

Road and Traffic Incidents

If you're renting a car in Tallinn or cycling through its streets, accidents can happen. Should you find yourself in a minor traffic accident, the general rule is to remain calm and contact the local authorities by dialing 112. If no one is injured and it's just a fender bender, exchanging information with the other party is the first step, but notifying the police is still required. They will document the incident, which is necessary for insurance claims.

If you're involved in a more serious incident, wait for the emergency services to arrive before attempting to move your vehicle or interfere with the scene. Estonia's traffic laws are taken seriously, and following the proper protocol will save you from future legal or insurance complications.

Weather-Related Emergencies

Winter in Tallinn can be cold and occasionally severe, with heavy snow or ice making some roads and sidewalks treacherous. If you find yourself stranded due to snow storms or severe weather, shelter in a safe, warm place. Hotels and cafes are common havens. Check weather forecasts daily, and in extreme cases, the local authorities issue warnings on public safety channels. Download a reliable weather app and keep track of the forecast to avoid getting caught in a storm.

No one likes to think about emergencies while traveling, but a bit of preparation goes a long way. Knowing how to handle a difficult situation will give you peace of mind so you can focus on enjoying the festive wonder of Tallinn. Save those essential emergency numbers, stay calm, and reach out for help when needed—you'll be well taken care of in this historic, yet modern city.

Chapter Ten

Where to Stay

Luxury Hotels

One of the luxurious and finest places to stay while exploring Tallinn is the Hotel Telegraaf, housed in a stunning 19th-century building. This five-star hotel blends modern comfort with historical elegance, featuring beautifully appointed rooms adorned with stylish furnishings. The hotel's location in the heart of the Old Town means you're just steps away from the bustling Christmas markets, where the aroma of roasted chestnuts wafts through the air.

For an unforgettable experience, don't miss the hotel's restaurant, Tchaikovsky, where you can indulge in exquisite local cuisine. Here, traditional Estonian flavors are artfully combined with contemporary techniques, creating a culinary delight that warms your soul as much as the surroundings.

Another gem is the St. Petersbourg Hotel, known for its boutique charm and sophisticated ambiance. Each room is uniquely designed, reflecting a blend of Russian and Estonian influences, offering a cozy yet opulent atmosphere. This hotel is perfect for couples looking to enjoy a romantic getaway. You can curl up by the fireplace in the hotel's lounge after a long day of exploring, sipping mulled wine while sharing stories of your adventures. The hotel's proximity to the Christmas market makes it convenient for late-night strolls under the twinkling lights.

If you want to immerse yourself in a truly lavish experience, the Schlössle Hotel offers history and modern luxury. Originally a medieval merchant's house, this hotel boasts elegant rooms with antique furnishings and state-of-the-art amenities. The intimate setting invites guests to unwind, and the on-site spa provides the perfect way to relax after a day of holiday shopping. You can enjoy a treatment using local ingredients, providing a refreshing touch to your stay.

Budget-Friendly Stays

Traveling during the Christmas season doesn't have to break the bank, and Tallinn offers several budget-friendly options that are both nice and welcoming. Picture this: you're wrapped up in a warm blanket after a day of wandering through festive markets, enjoying a warm drink in your quaint accommodation. One of the best places to start your budget-friendly adventure is at The Monk's Bunk, a hostel that offers both dormitory-style and private rooms. It's a social hub where you can meet fellow travelers, share stories over breakfast, and even partake in the occasional game night. The laid-back atmosphere makes it easy to settle in, and the hostel is conveniently located near the Old Town, so you can easily explore the area.

For those seeking a bit more privacy without sacrificing comfort, Tallinn City Hostel is a great choice. This cozy establishment features clean, simple rooms and a friendly staff that goes above and beyond to make you feel at home. The communal kitchen is perfect for whipping up a warm breakfast before heading out into the cold. And the best part? It's just a short walk from all the major sights, including the Town Hall Square and its festive atmosphere.

If you're looking for a unique experience, consider Kalev Spa Hotel & Waterpark. Not only does it offer comfortable accommodations, but it also features a water park, perfect for families or anyone looking to have a little fun indoors. After a day of exploring, unwind in the spa facilities or splash around in the pool—after all, a little adventure adds to your travel story. Plus, it's located near the heart of the city, so you won't miss out on the festive happenings.

For those who prefer a homey feel, Airbnb options in Tallinn provide a myriad of cozy apartments and houses to choose from. Imagine staying in a quaint apartment in the Old Town, complete with a fully equipped kitchen where you can prepare a festive dinner using local ingredients you picked up at the market. This flexibility lets you experience Tallinn like a local, giving you the freedom to create your holiday traditions while enjoying the comforts of home.

Vacation Rentals

If you're planning a getaway to this enchanting destination during Christmas, opting for a vacation rental can make all the difference. Here's your guide to finding the perfect place to stay while experiencing Tallinn like a local.

Christmas Cottages

If you're looking for that homey feel during your stay, Tallinn offers a selection of delightful cottages that provide warmth and comfort. Imagine settling into a snug wooden cabin, complete with a crackling fireplace and twinkling fairy lights. One standout is the Püha Cottage, located just a short drive from the city center. This quaint retreat is surrounded by pristine nature, making it ideal for those seeking tranquility away from the hustle and bustle. With modern amenities and rustic decor, you can truly unwind while still being close enough to explore Tallinn's attractions.

For a more traditional experience, consider Rae Cottage. Nestled within the historic district, it combines modern comfort with old-world aesthetics. You'll feel as if you've stepped back in time, yet have all the conveniences at your fingertips. The best part? You can stroll through the nearby Christmas market in Town Hall Square after a warm, comforting meal prepared in your fully equipped kitchen. Nothing beats a cozy night in, sipping hot cocoa while enjoying the snow gently falling outside your window.

Boutique Hotels

If you prefer a touch of elegance during your holiday, Tallinn boasts a range of boutique hotels that blend local culture with contemporary design. One such gem is the Hotel Telegraaf, located in a beautifully restored building dating back to the 19th century. This hotel is perfect for those who appreciate fine details and want to soak in the history of the city. With a lavish spa, gourmet dining options, and a prime location just steps away from the bustling market, it's an ideal base for your festive adventure.

Another fantastic option is The Gotthard Hotel, which perfectly captures Tallinn's medieval essence while offering modern luxuries. Each room is uniquely decorated, reflecting the rich history of the city. After a day of exploring the cobbled streets adorned with twinkling lights, returning to this boutique haven feels like a warm embrace. Enjoy a delightful breakfast spread before heading out to witness the beauty of Tallinn in winter.

Living Like a Local

Staying in a vacation rental or boutique hotel in Tallinn gives you the opportunity to be truly involved in the local culture. You can visit a nearby grocery store to gather ingredients for a traditional Estonian feast, or take a leisurely stroll through the quaint neighborhoods, discovering hidden cafes where you can sip on local brews. It's the little things that make your stay memorable—like chatting with a friendly barista about the best places to visit during the festive season.

Don't miss the chance to explore Tallinn's unique Christmas traditions while you're here. Many rental homes are located close to local markets, where you can experience the excitement of the holiday season firsthand. Engaging with local artisans, sampling traditional dishes, and participating in festivities will make your experience all the more enriching.

Tips for Choosing Your Perfect Stay

When selecting a vacation rental or boutique hotel in Tallinn, consider your priorities. Are you looking for a quiet retreat or a central location close to the festivities? Check online reviews for insights into cleanliness, hospitality, and amenities. Booking in advance is highly recommended during the holiday season to secure your ideal accommodation.

Additionally, be sure to check if your chosen place offers holiday-specific packages or activities. Some rentals may even provide festive decorations or local guides that can help you navigate Tallinn's seasonal offerings, ensuring your trip is memorable for all the right reasons.

Booking Tips

Planning a trip to Tallinn during the festive season is exciting, and securing the best deals can make your experience even more enjoyable. Let's talk about some friendly tips to help you navigate the booking process like a seasoned traveler.

Timing is Everything

When it comes to booking your accommodations and activities, timing plays a crucial role. For the Christmas season, it's best to start looking at least three to six months or less in advance. This allows you to snag the most sought-after hotels, especially those with a view of the enchanting Christmas markets. Keep in mind that Tallinn can get crowded during the holiday season, so early bookings can save you from the stress of last-minute planning.

Flexible Dates

If your schedule allows it, being flexible with your travel dates can lead to significant savings. Try searching for flights and hotels a few days before or after your preferred travel dates. Sometimes, a simple shift can drop the prices significantly. Additionally, consider traveling mid-week rather than on weekends, as this is when you're likely to find better deals.

Comparison Shopping

Use hotel and flight comparison websites to sift through the options available to you. Websites like Skyscanner or Kayak can help you find the best prices for flights, while platforms like Booking.com and Expedia allow you to filter through hotels based on your preferences. It's a great way to compare different offerings and find that perfect spot that fits your budget and needs.

Sign Up for Alerts

Don't underestimate the power of travel alert emails. Many travel websites offer alerts that notify you when prices drop for your selected routes or accommodations. This is an easy way to keep track of deals without constantly searching, giving you a better chance at snagging those sought-after prices.

Local Websites and Offers

Sometimes, the best deals are found on local Estonian websites. Consider checking platforms like Visit Estonia or local hotel websites directly. They often have exclusive offers or packages during the holiday season that might not be available on international sites.

Consider Alternative Accommodations

If hotels are not fitting your budget, think outside the box! Airbnb or local guesthouses can provide unique experiences at more reasonable prices. Imagine staying in a cozy apartment right in the heart of the Old Town, with the markets just a short stroll away.

Plan Activities Early

Finally, don't forget to book your Christmas activities in advance. Popular events like Christmas concerts and guided tours often sell out quickly. Secure your spots early to ensure you don't miss out on the experiences that make your trip memorable.

Conclusion

As you prepare to embark on your journey to Tallinn this Christmas season, take a moment to savor the excitement bubbling within you. The Estonian capital truly transforms into a wonderland during this time, and there's no better way to experience it than through the stories and traditions that fill its winter nights.

Throughout this guide, we've ventured together through Tallinn's holiday spirit. You've discovered the best markets, where artisans showcase their handcrafted gifts, perfect for those on your nice list. You've explored mouthwatering dishes that showcase the flavors of Estonia—dishes that tell their own stories of history and culture. It's these moments of indulgence and exploration that make your trip memorable and, dare I say, heartwarming.

Start your day with a stroll through the Old Town, its medieval architectures and whispering tales of centuries. You might hear a street musician strumming a festive tune or catch a glimpse of children gleefully racing down snow-covered hills. This is not just a destination; it's an experience woven into the fabric of the holiday season. And let's not forget about the enchanting Christmas lights illuminating every corner of the city. As you meander through the narrow streets, each step brings a new discovery—a quirky café, a hidden courtyard, or an impressive view from a hilltop.

And for those traveling with family, Tallinn offers endless activities to keep everyone entertained. From the joyful atmosphere of the Christmas markets to the engaging experiences at the Estonian Open Air Museum, your family can bond over the fun of trying local delicacies or participating in interactive workshops. These shared experiences will create lasting memories that you'll cherish long after your trip ends.

If you find yourself yearning for a bit of adventure, consider venturing beyond the city limits. The nearby Lahemaa National Park beckons with its untouched beauty, and there's nothing quite like a day spent hiking through snow-dusted trails or sledding down gentle slopes. The peacefulness of nature provides a perfect counterpoint to the hustle and bustle of the city, offering you a chance to reconnect with your surroundings and appreciate the serene beauty of Estonia's winter landscape.

As you finalize your travel plans, keep in mind the practical tips shared in this guide—packing appropriately for the cold, budgeting wisely, and familiarizing yourself with local customs. These insights are designed to ensure your trip goes smoothly, allowing you to focus on enjoying every moment.

Tallinn is a city steeped in history and alive with festive spirit, and your adventure here will be one for the books. So, embrace the sights, the sounds, and the tastes that Tallinn has to offer. This Christmas season, let the warmth of the local traditions envelop you and invite you to be a part of their stories.

Your journey awaits, and it promises to be filled with delightful surprises. Safe travels, and may your time in Tallinn bring you joy, wonder, and cherished memories that last a lifetime!

Printed in Great Britain
by Amazon